My Life Beyond
NEUROFIBROMATOSIS

A Mayo Clinic patient story
by Hey Gee and G.W. Page

Foreword

Hi! I'm G.W. and I was born with neurofibromatosis. We say NF, for short, since the full name is hard to pronounce. Having NF means sometimes I get headaches, random pains in my arms, legs and neck, and bumps and itchiness on my skin. I also go to more clinic appointments than most kids. That's because NF causes tumors to grow on nerves in the body. Since there is no cure for NF — yet — my doctors keep an extra close eye on me to be sure we find any new nerve pain, tumors or eye problems before they get to be a problem. I have a lot of MRIs, which are tests where big cameras in the hospital take pictures of the inside of my body. I have to lie very still for these pictures. The MRI machine can be really noisy. It makes a loud thumping noise. You can wear earplugs so it isn't so loud. The MRI doesn't hurt, though. You won't feel anything during it. I've had 20 so far!

My mom and dad run a nonprofit organization for neurofibromatosis. They've been doing it since I was little to help other people with NF and work with researchers to find a cure. My dad meets with scientists from all over the world and people who work for the U.S. government to find new medicines and treatments for NF. I am not afraid of NF. It helps to know my doctors and my family are here to help me.

I named the character in this book Leo because it means lion, and "Little Lion" is the nickname my mom and dad have always had for me. They say it's because I am brave. Remember, there are very smart people working very hard to find new treatments and a cure for NF.

G.W. Page

"

BE BRAVE AND
READY FOR ANYTHING

"

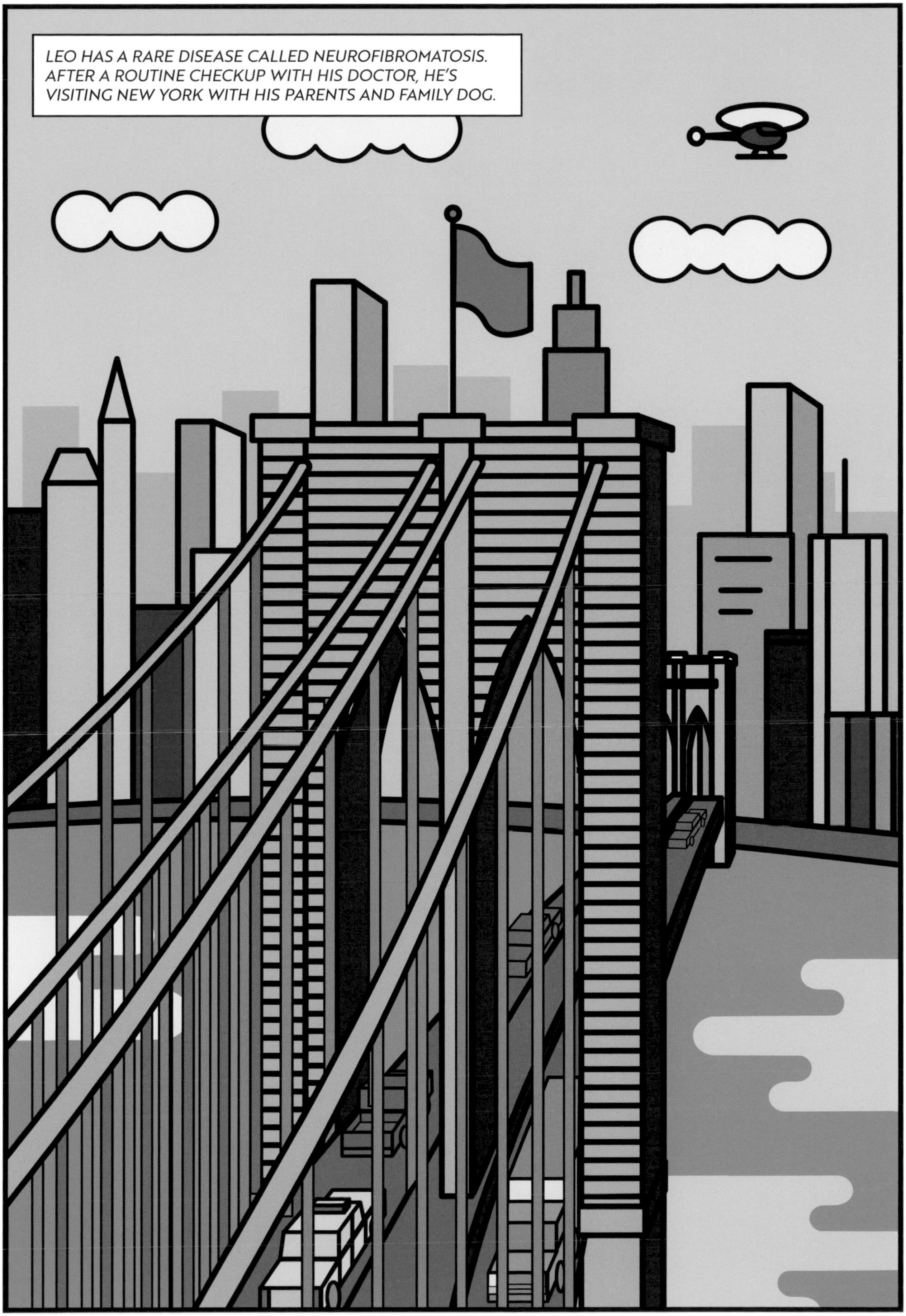
LEO HAS A RARE DISEASE CALLED NEUROFIBROMATOSIS. AFTER A ROUTINE CHECKUP WITH HIS DOCTOR, HE'S VISITING NEW YORK WITH HIS PARENTS AND FAMILY DOG.

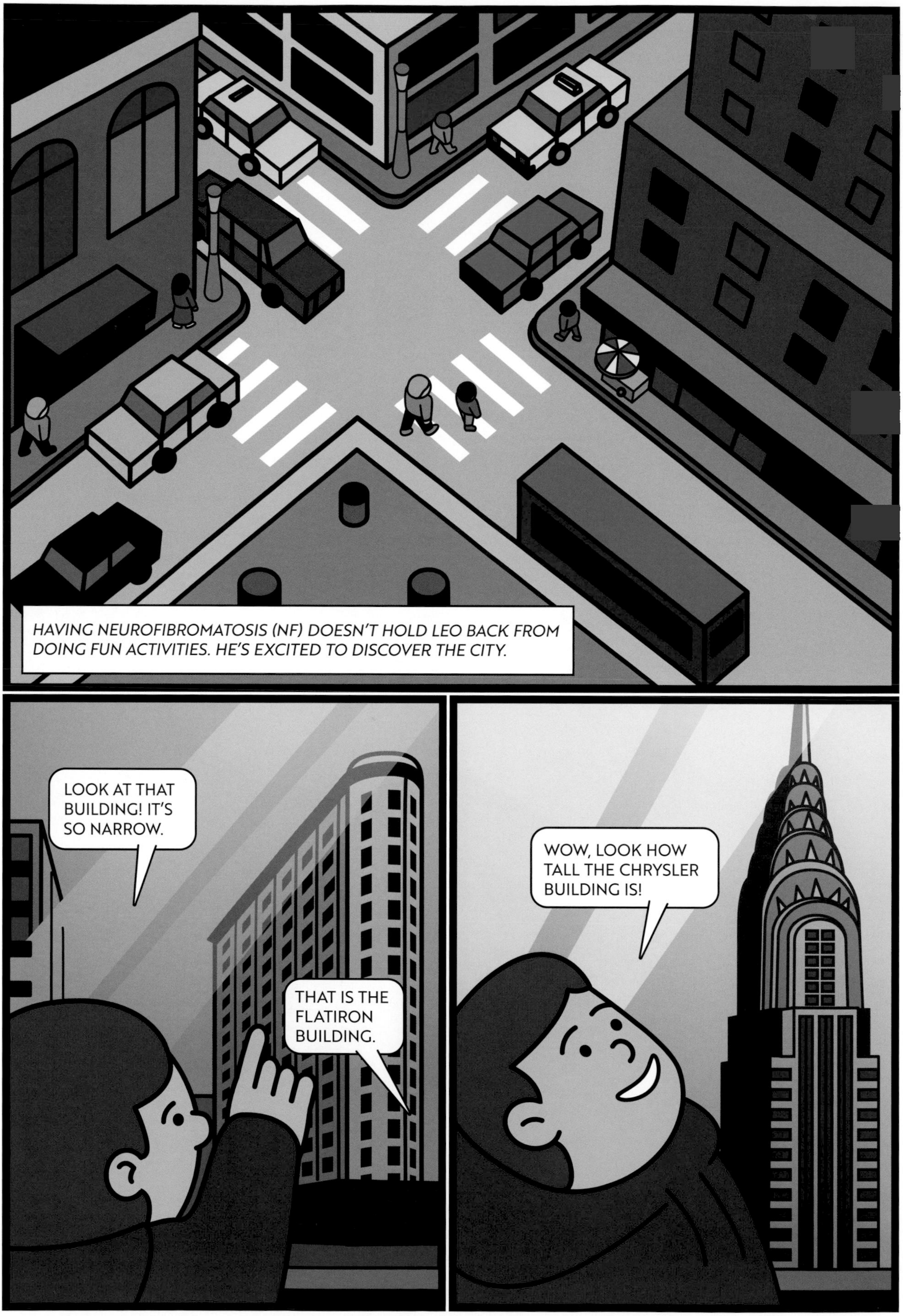
HAVING NEUROFIBROMATOSIS (NF) DOESN'T HOLD LEO BACK FROM DOING FUN ACTIVITIES. HE'S EXCITED TO DISCOVER THE CITY.
LOOK AT THAT BUILDING! IT'S SO NARROW.
THAT IS THE FLATIRON BUILDING.
WOW, LOOK HOW TALL THE CHRYSLER BUILDING IS!

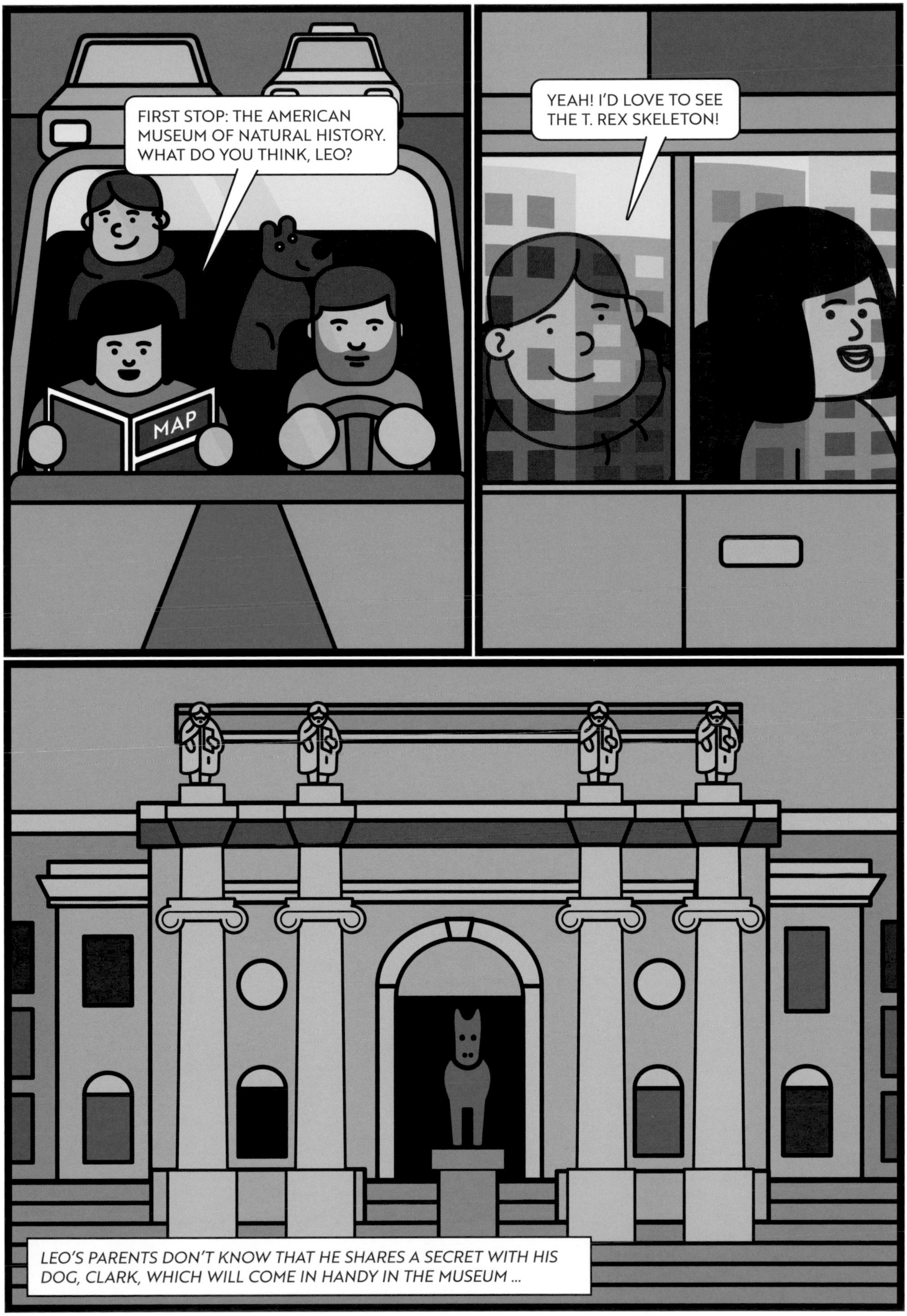
FIRST STOP: THE AMERICAN MUSEUM OF NATURAL HISTORY. WHAT DO YOU THINK, LEO?
MAP
YEAH! I'D LOVE TO SEE THE T. REX SKELETON!
LEO'S PARENTS DON'T KNOW THAT HE SHARES A SECRET WITH HIS DOG, CLARK, WHICH WILL COME IN HANDY IN THE MUSEUM ...

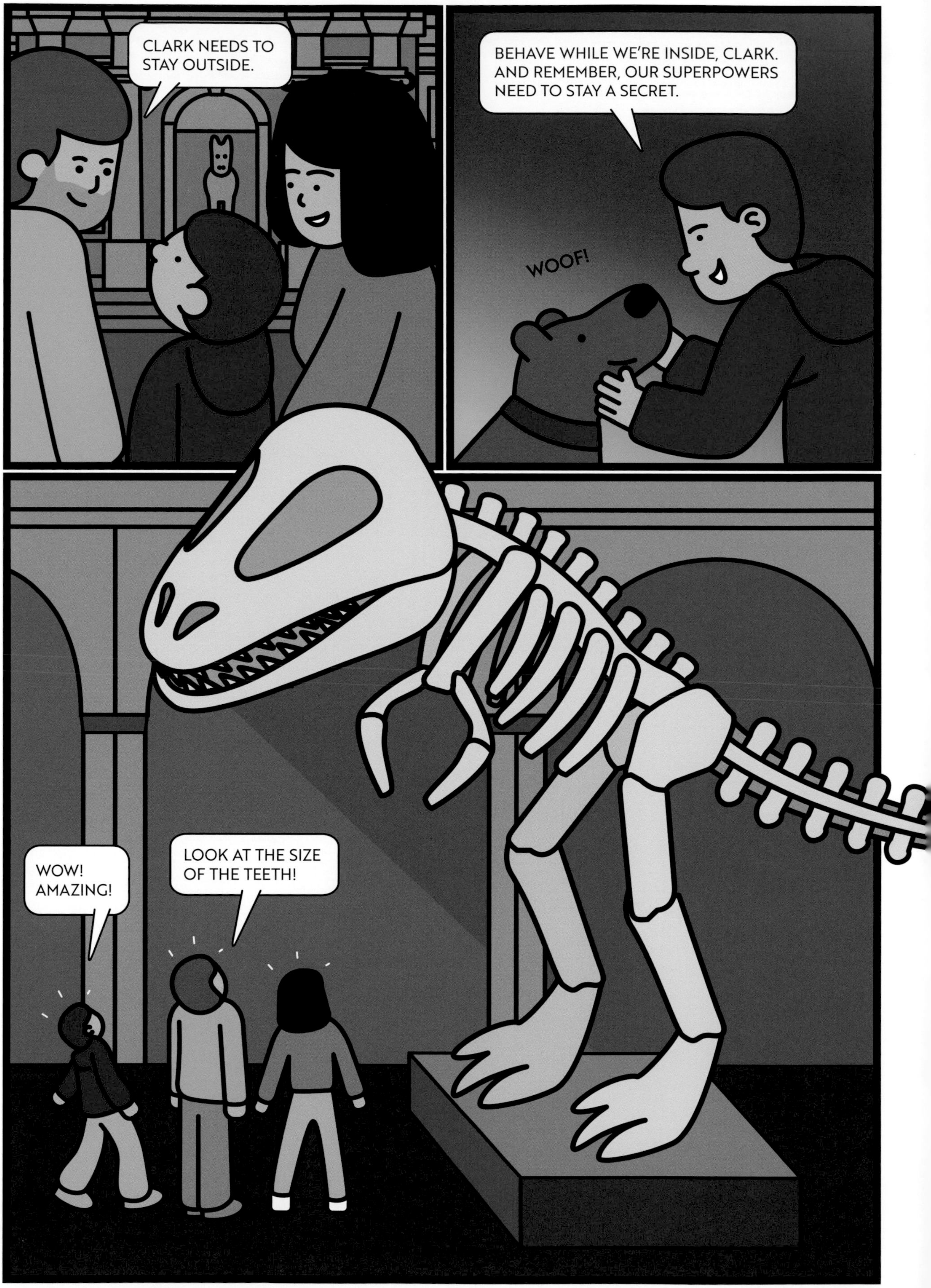
CLARK NEEDS TO STAY OUTSIDE.
BEHAVE WHILE WE'RE INSIDE, CLARK. AND REMEMBER, OUR SUPERPOWERS NEED TO STAY A SECRET.
WOOF!
WOW! AMAZING!
LOOK AT THE SIZE OF THE TEETH!

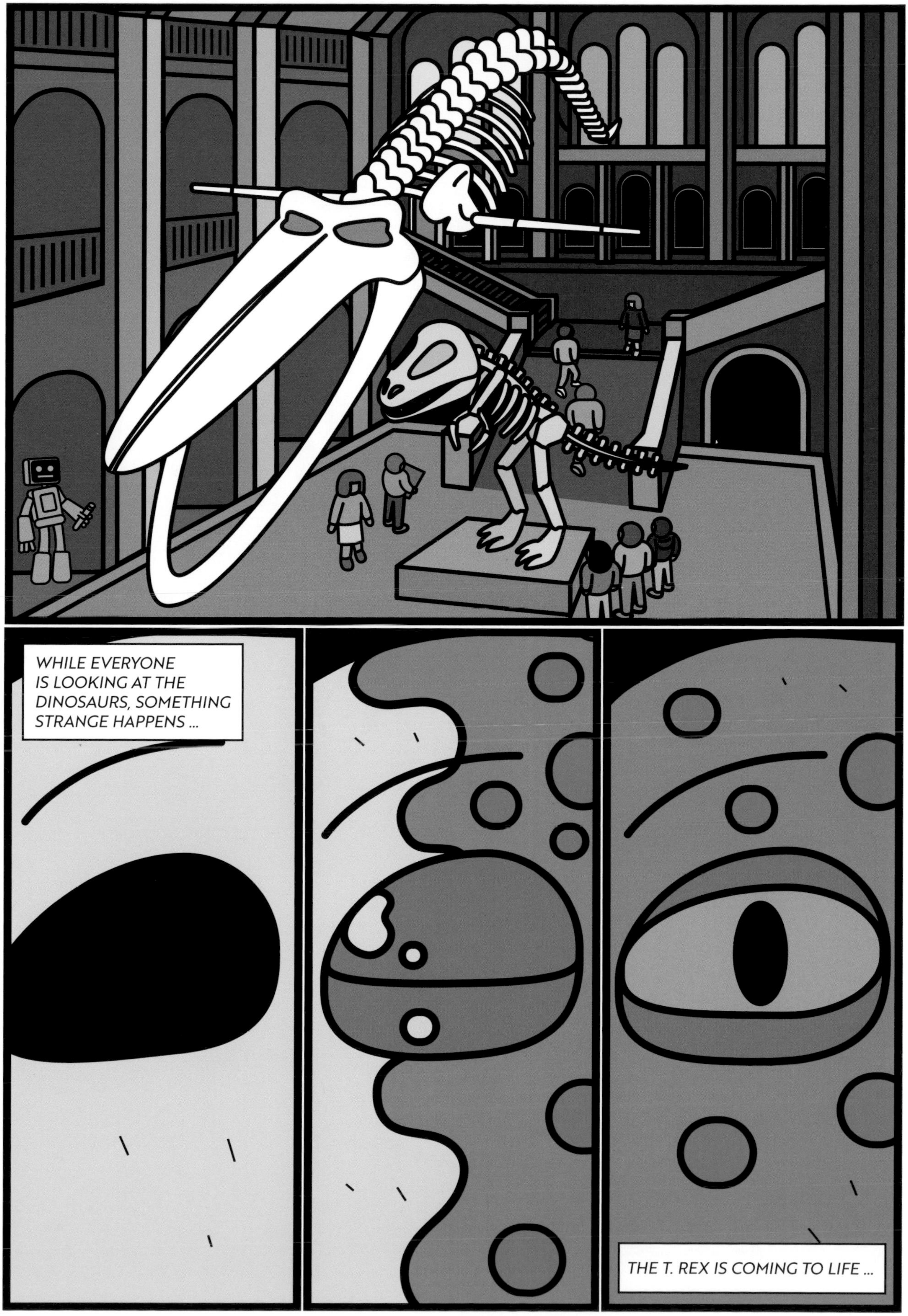
WHILE EVERYONE IS LOOKING AT THE DINOSAURS, SOMETHING STRANGE HAPPENS ...
THE T. REX IS COMING TO LIFE ...

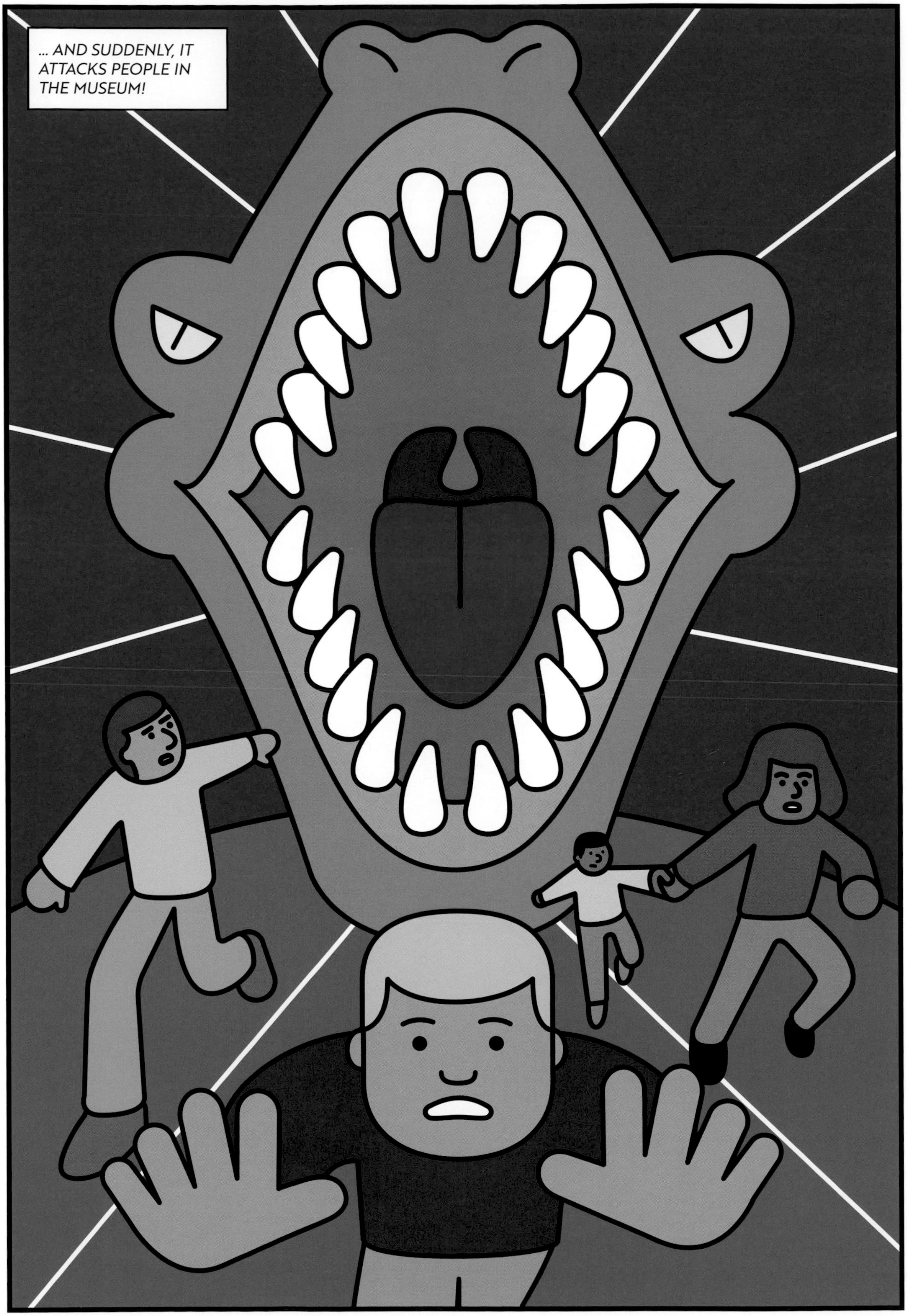
... AND SUDDENLY, IT ATTACKS PEOPLE IN THE MUSEUM!

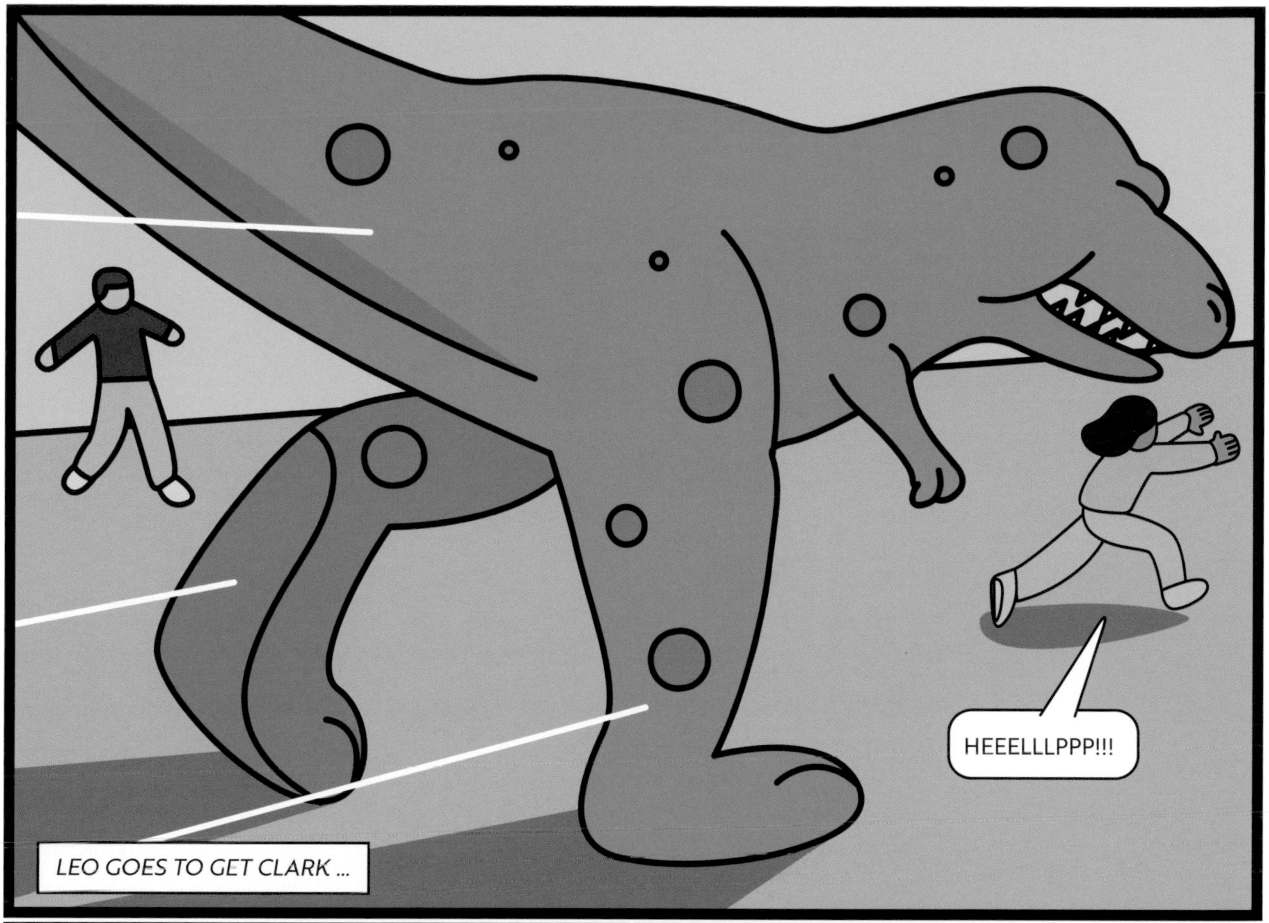
HEEELLLPPP!!!
LEO GOES TO GET CLARK ...

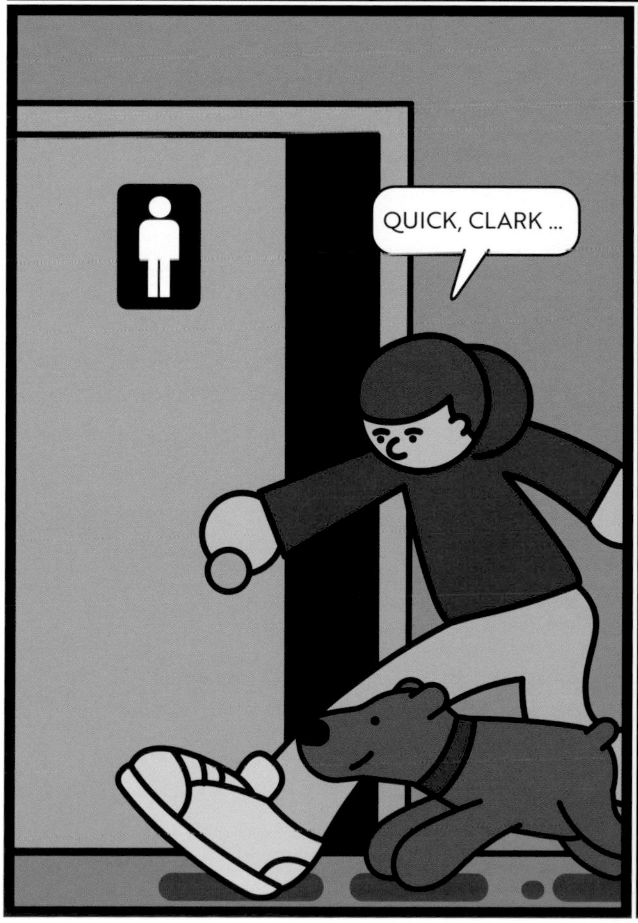
QUICK, CLARK ...

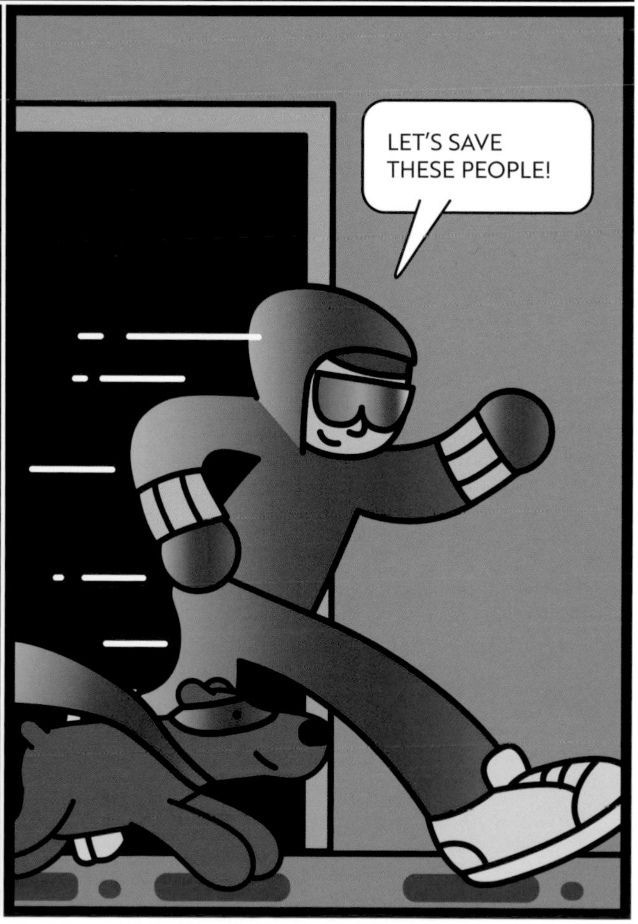
LET'S SAVE THESE PEOPLE!

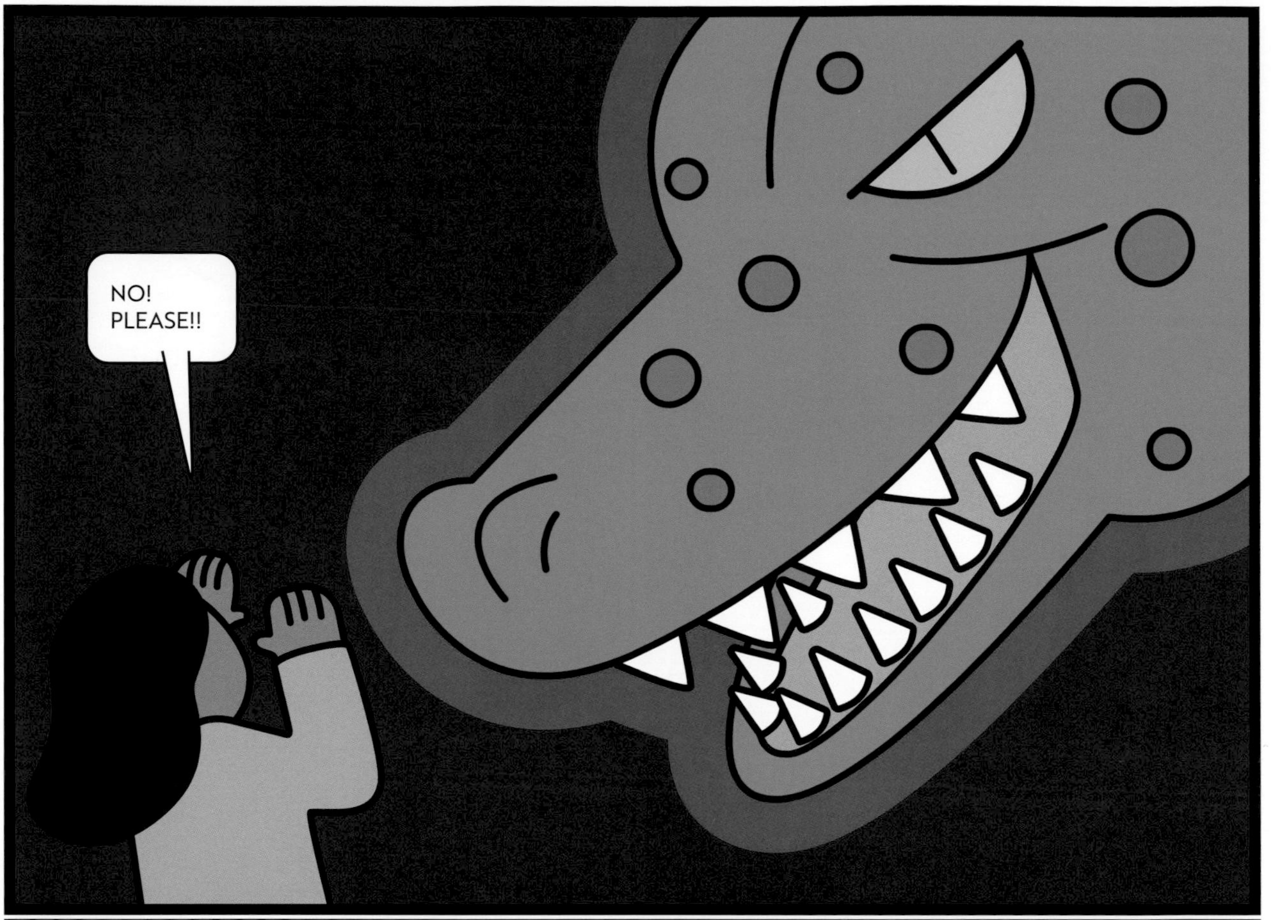
NO!
PLEASE!!

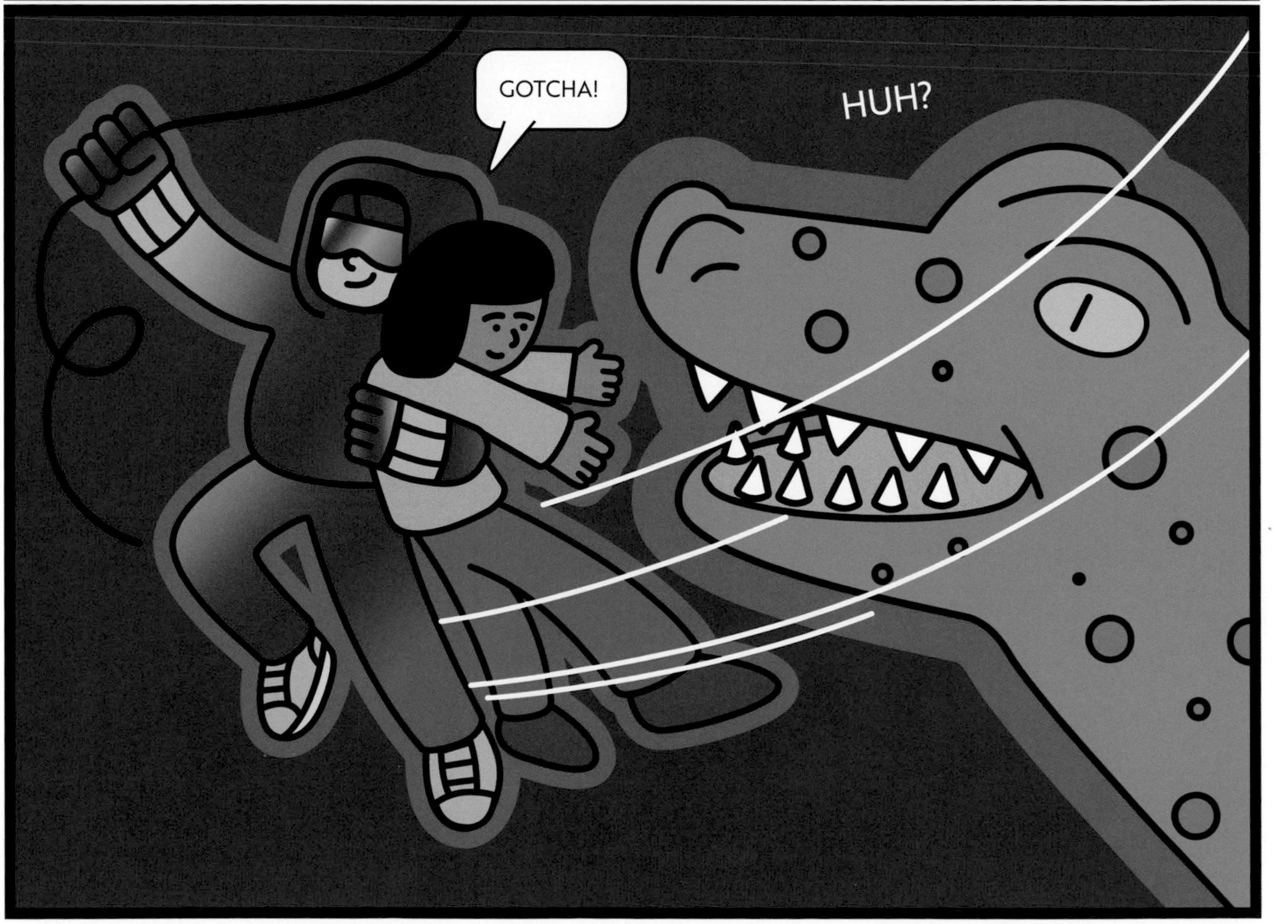
GOTCHA!
HUH?

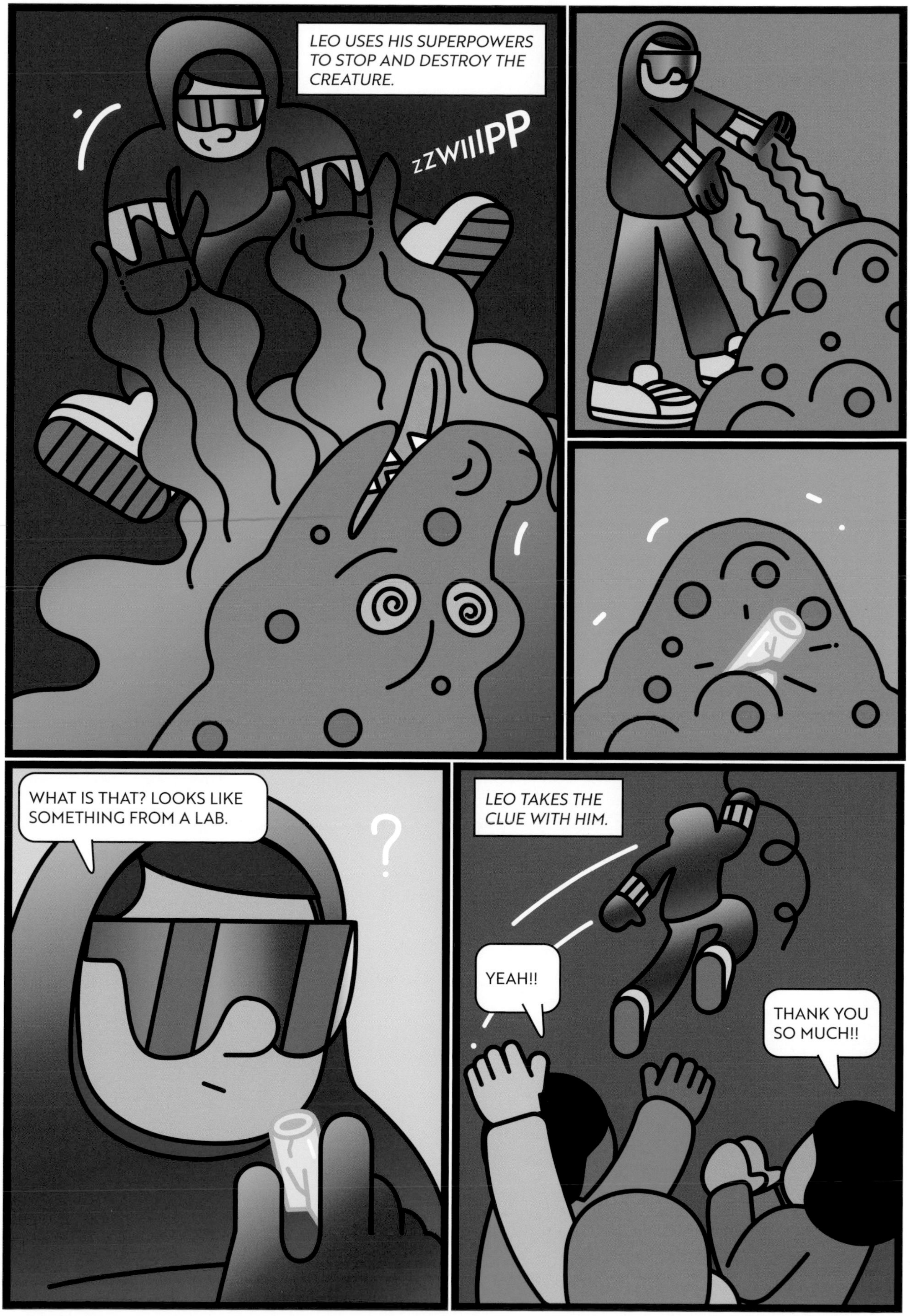
LEO USES HIS SUPERPOWERS TO STOP AND DESTROY THE CREATURE.
ZZWIIIPP
WHAT IS THAT? LOOKS LIKE SOMETHING FROM A LAB.
?
LEO TAKES THE CLUE WITH HIM.
YEAH!!
THANK YOU SO MUCH!!

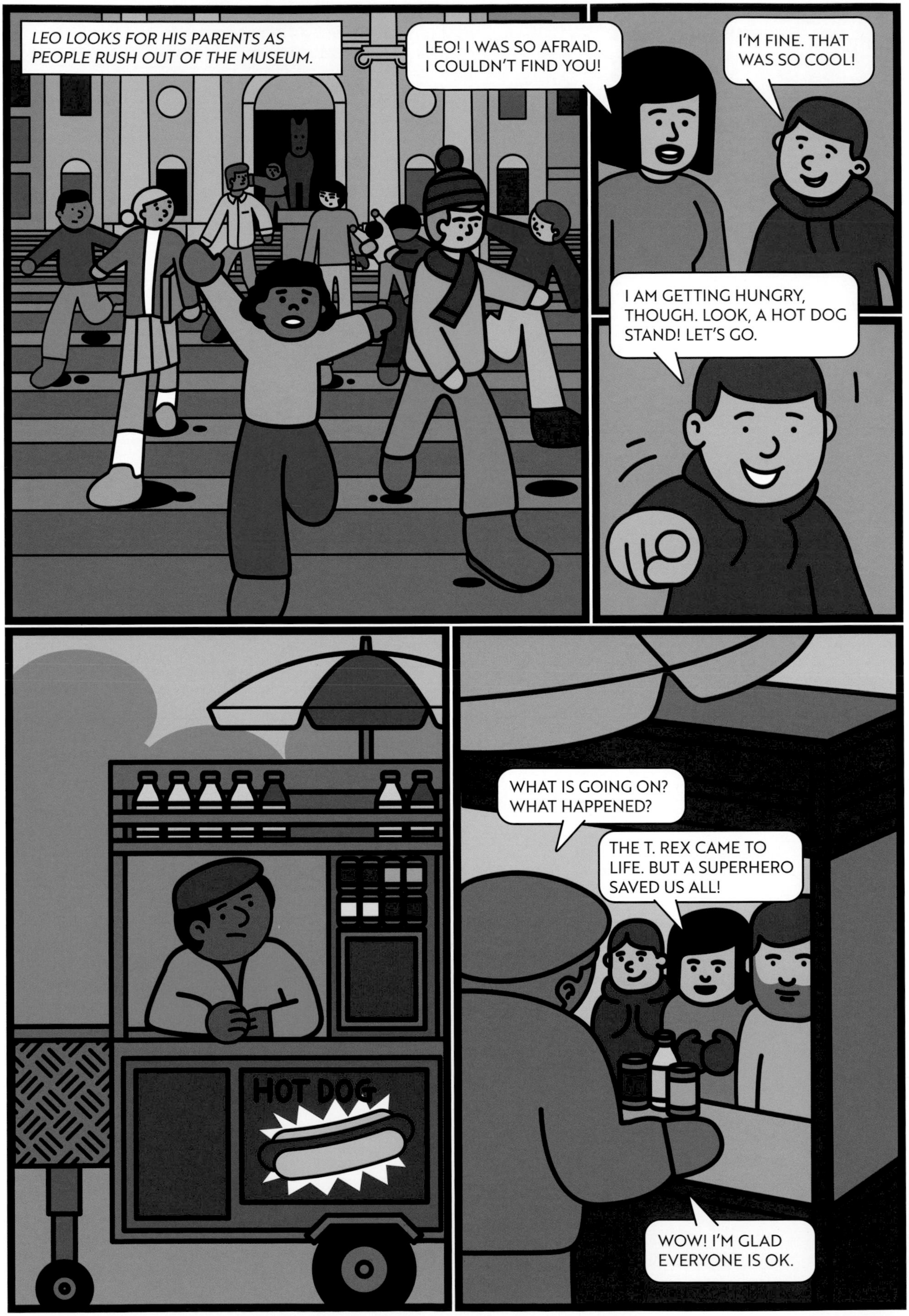
LEO LOOKS FOR HIS PARENTS AS PEOPLE RUSH OUT OF THE MUSEUM.
LEO! I WAS SO AFRAID. I COULDN'T FIND YOU!
I'M FINE. THAT WAS SO COOL!
I AM GETTING HUNGRY, THOUGH. LOOK, A HOT DOG STAND! LET'S GO.
HOT DOG
WHAT IS GOING ON? WHAT HAPPENED?
THE T. REX CAME TO LIFE. BUT A SUPERHERO SAVED US ALL!
WOW! I'M GLAD EVERYONE IS OK.

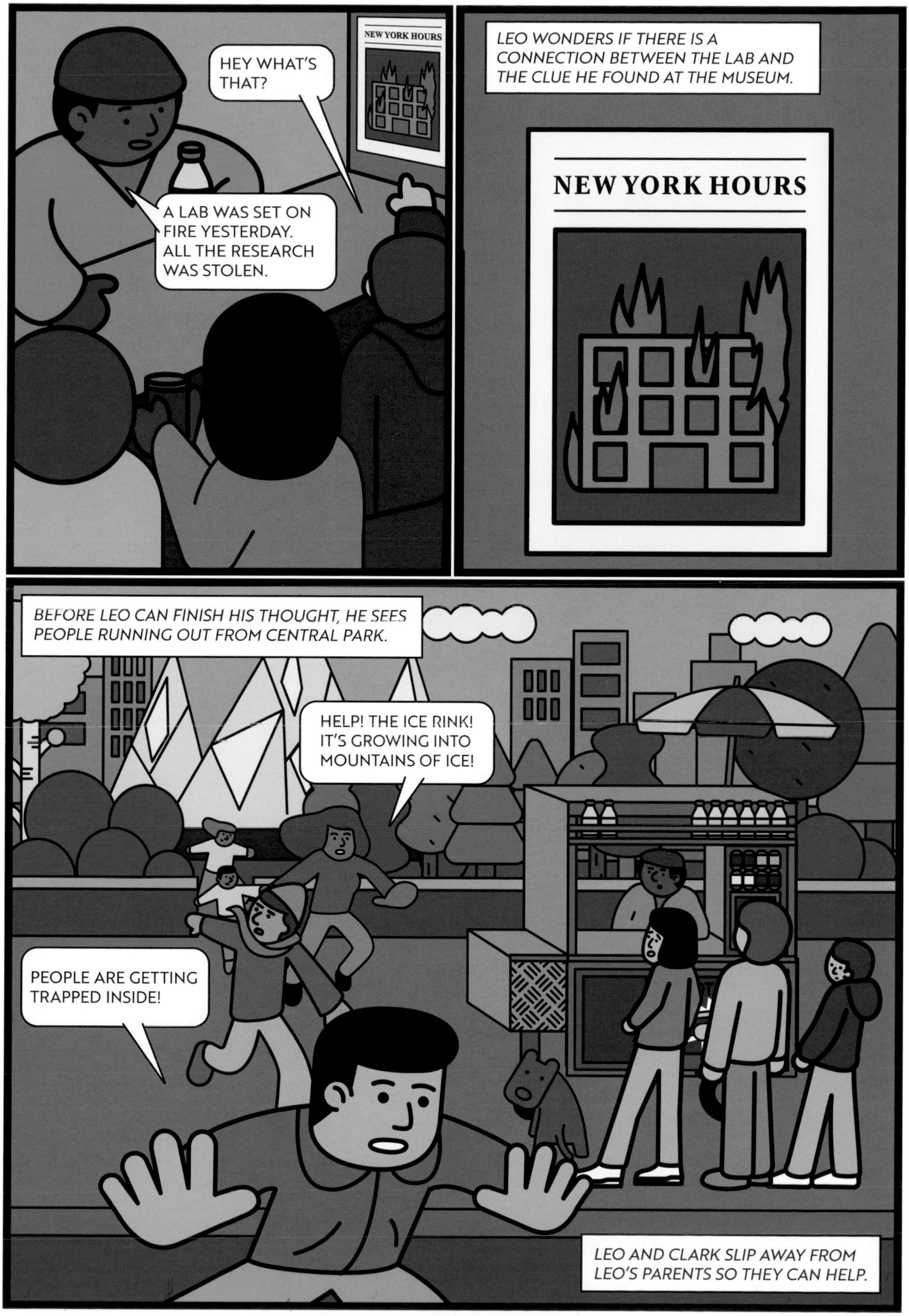
HEY WHAT'S THAT?
A LAB WAS SET ON FIRE YESTERDAY. ALL THE RESEARCH WAS STOLEN.
NEW YORK HOURS
LEO WONDERS IF THERE IS A CONNECTION BETWEEN THE LAB AND THE CLUE HE FOUND AT THE MUSEUM.
NEW YORK HOURS
BEFORE LEO CAN FINISH HIS THOUGHT, HE SEES PEOPLE RUNNING OUT FROM CENTRAL PARK.
HELP! THE ICE RINK! IT'S GROWING INTO MOUNTAINS OF ICE!
PEOPLE ARE GETTING TRAPPED INSIDE!
LEO AND CLARK SLIP AWAY FROM LEO'S PARENTS SO THEY CAN HELP.

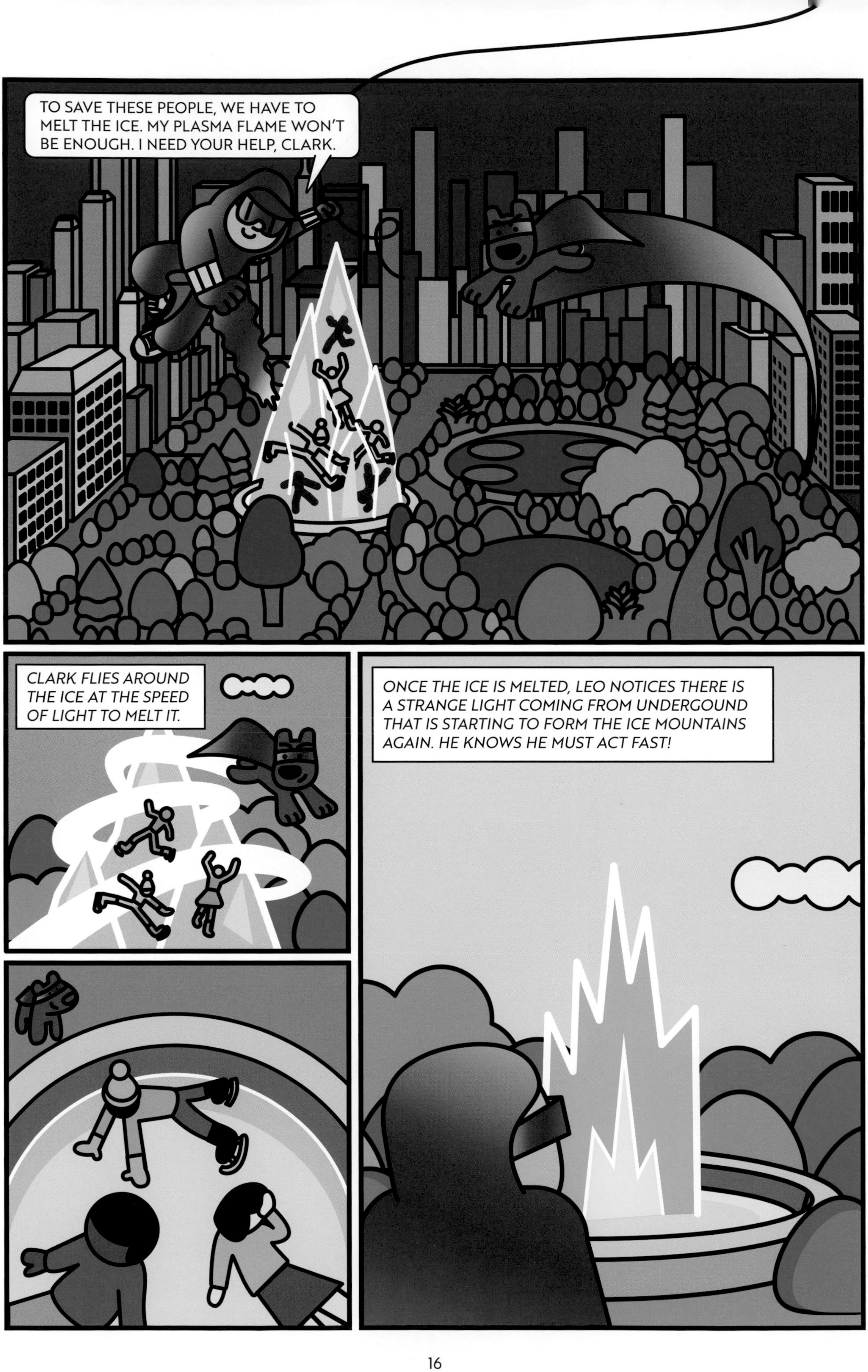
TO SAVE THESE PEOPLE, WE HAVE TO MELT THE ICE. MY PLASMA FLAME WON'T BE ENOUGH. I NEED YOUR HELP, CLARK.
CLARK FLIES AROUND THE ICE AT THE SPEED OF LIGHT TO MELT IT.
ONCE THE ICE IS MELTED, LEO NOTICES THERE IS A STRANGE LIGHT COMING FROM UNDERGOUND THAT IS STARTING TO FORM THE ICE MOUNTAINS AGAIN. HE KNOWS HE MUST ACT FAST!

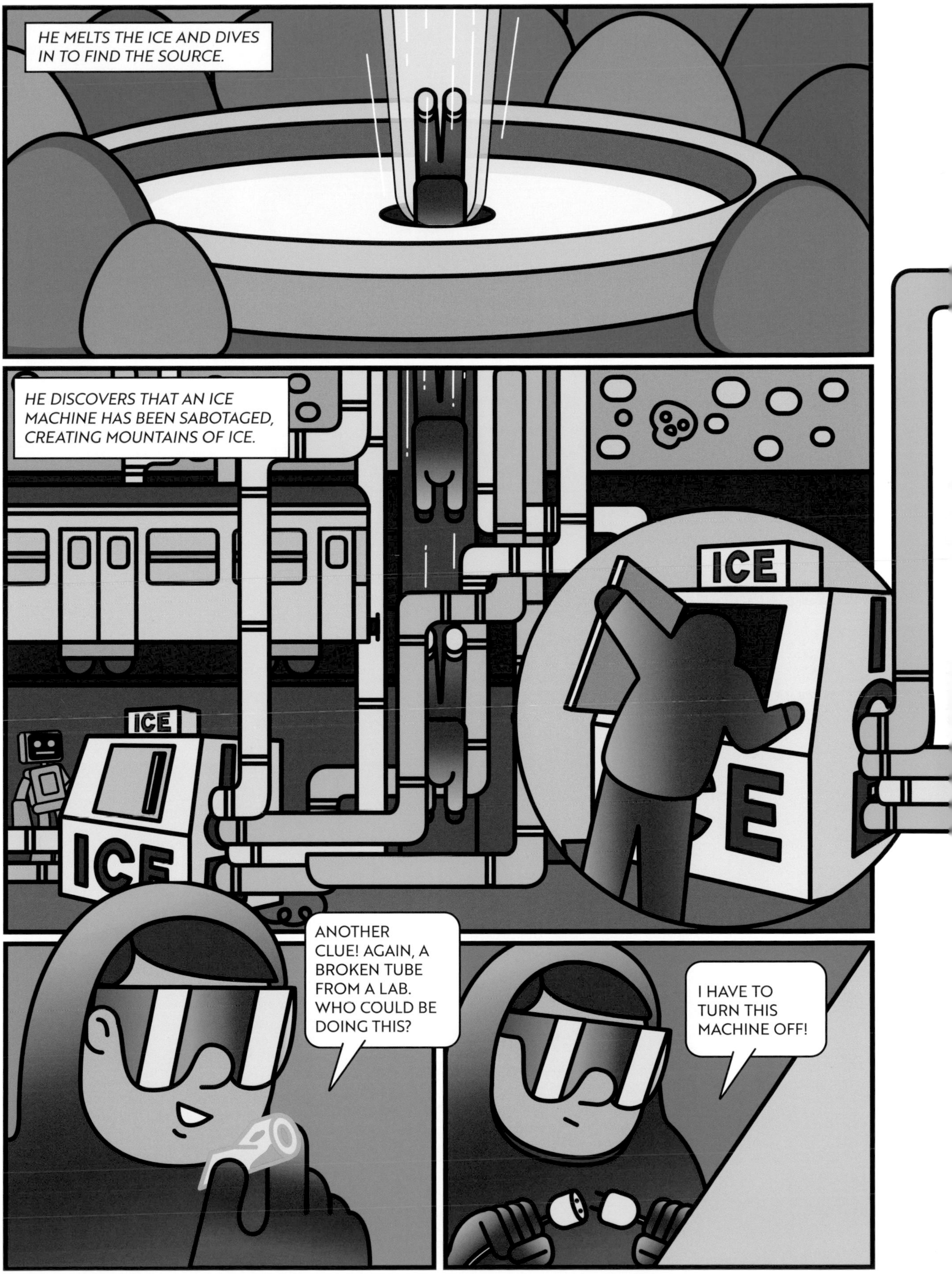
HE MELTS THE ICE AND DIVES IN TO FIND THE SOURCE.
HE DISCOVERS THAT AN ICE MACHINE HAS BEEN SABOTAGED, CREATING MOUNTAINS OF ICE.
ICE
ICE
ICE
ANOTHER CLUE! AGAIN, A BROKEN TUBE FROM A LAB. WHO COULD BE DOING THIS?
I HAVE TO TURN THIS MACHINE OFF!

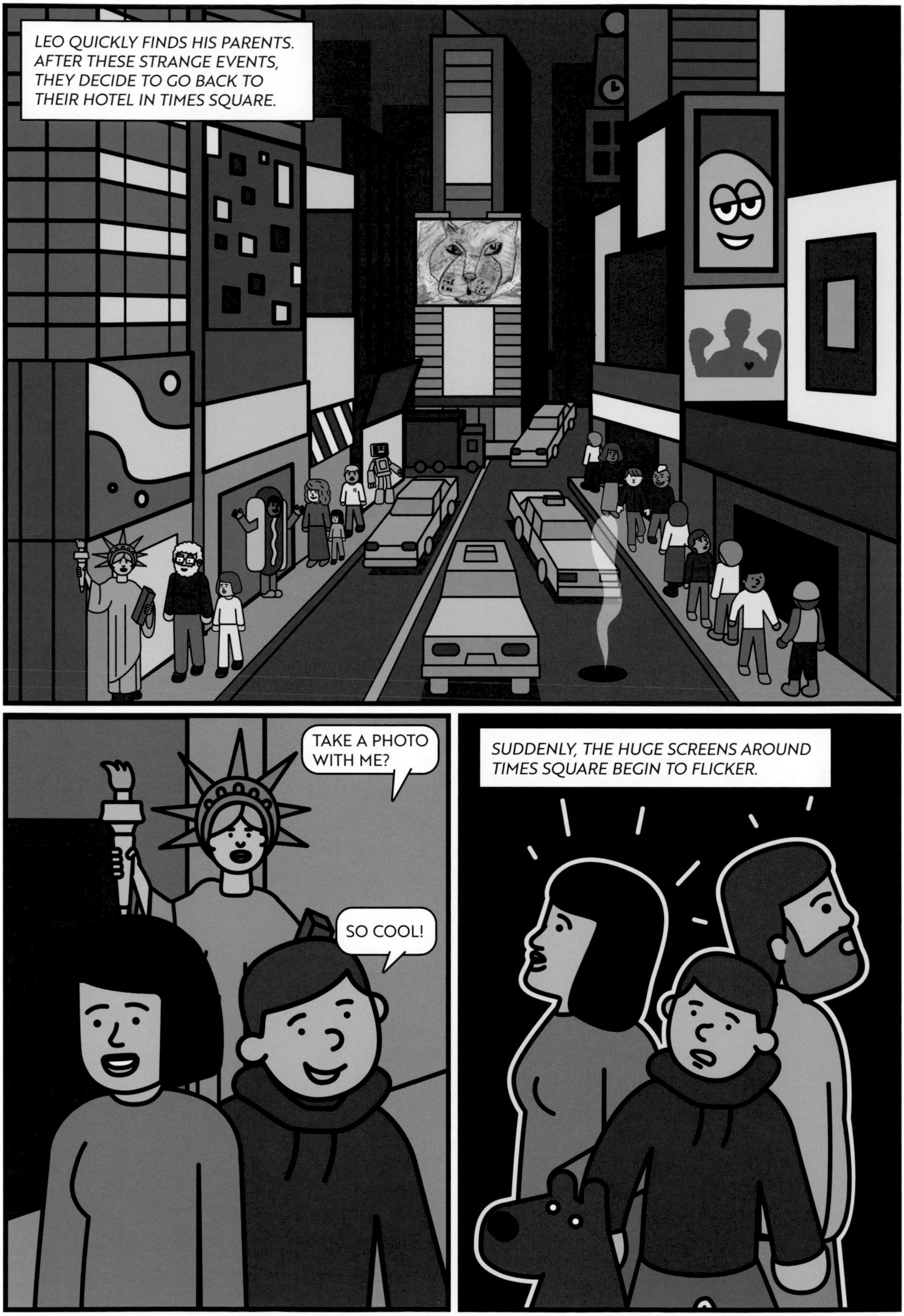
LEO QUICKLY FINDS HIS PARENTS. AFTER THESE STRANGE EVENTS, THEY DECIDE TO GO BACK TO THEIR HOTEL IN TIMES SQUARE.
TAKE A PHOTO WITH ME?
SO COOL!
SUDDENLY, THE HUGE SCREENS AROUND TIMES SQUARE BEGIN TO FLICKER.

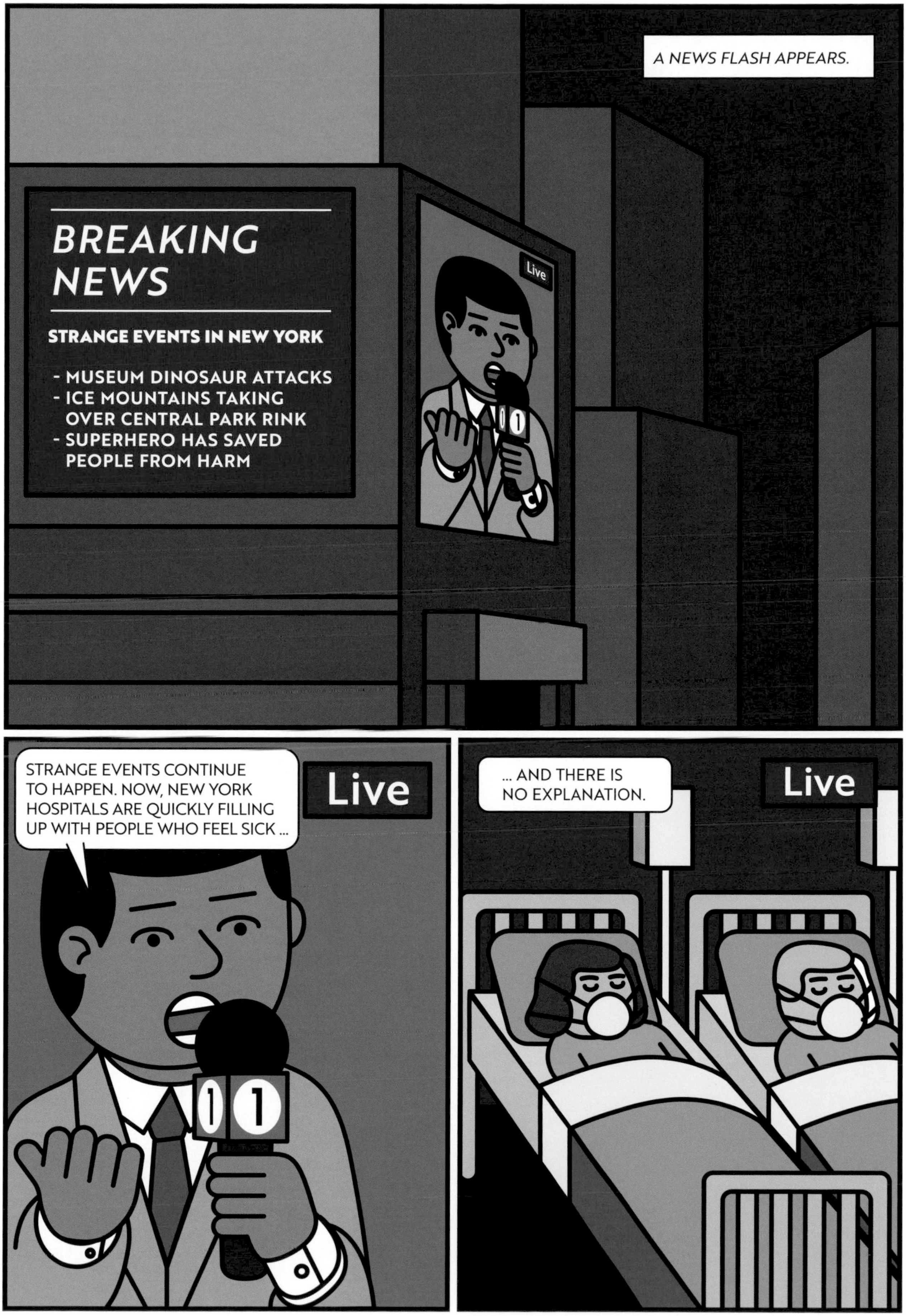
A NEWS FLASH APPEARS.
BREAKING NEWS
STRANGE EVENTS IN NEW YORK
- MUSEUM DINOSAUR ATTACKS
- ICE MOUNTAINS TAKING OVER CENTRAL PARK RINK
- SUPERHERO HAS SAVED PEOPLE FROM HARM
Live
STRANGE EVENTS CONTINUE TO HAPPEN. NOW, NEW YORK HOSPITALS ARE QUICKLY FILLING UP WITH PEOPLE WHO FEEL SICK ...
Live
... AND THERE IS NO EXPLANATION.
Live

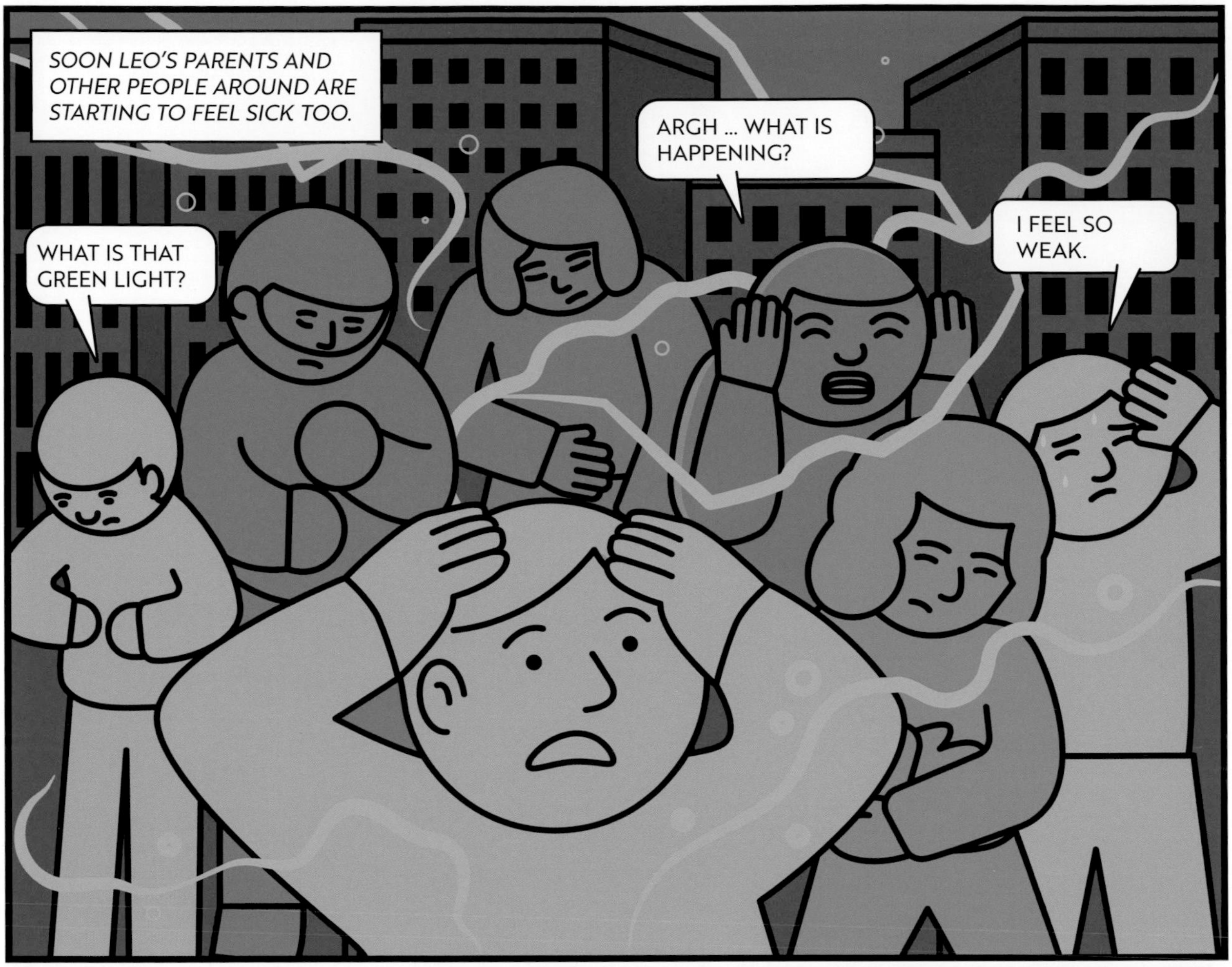
SOON LEO'S PARENTS AND OTHER PEOPLE AROUND ARE STARTING TO FEEL SICK TOO.
WHAT IS THAT GREEN LIGHT?
ARGH ... WHAT IS HAPPENING?
I FEEL SO WEAK.

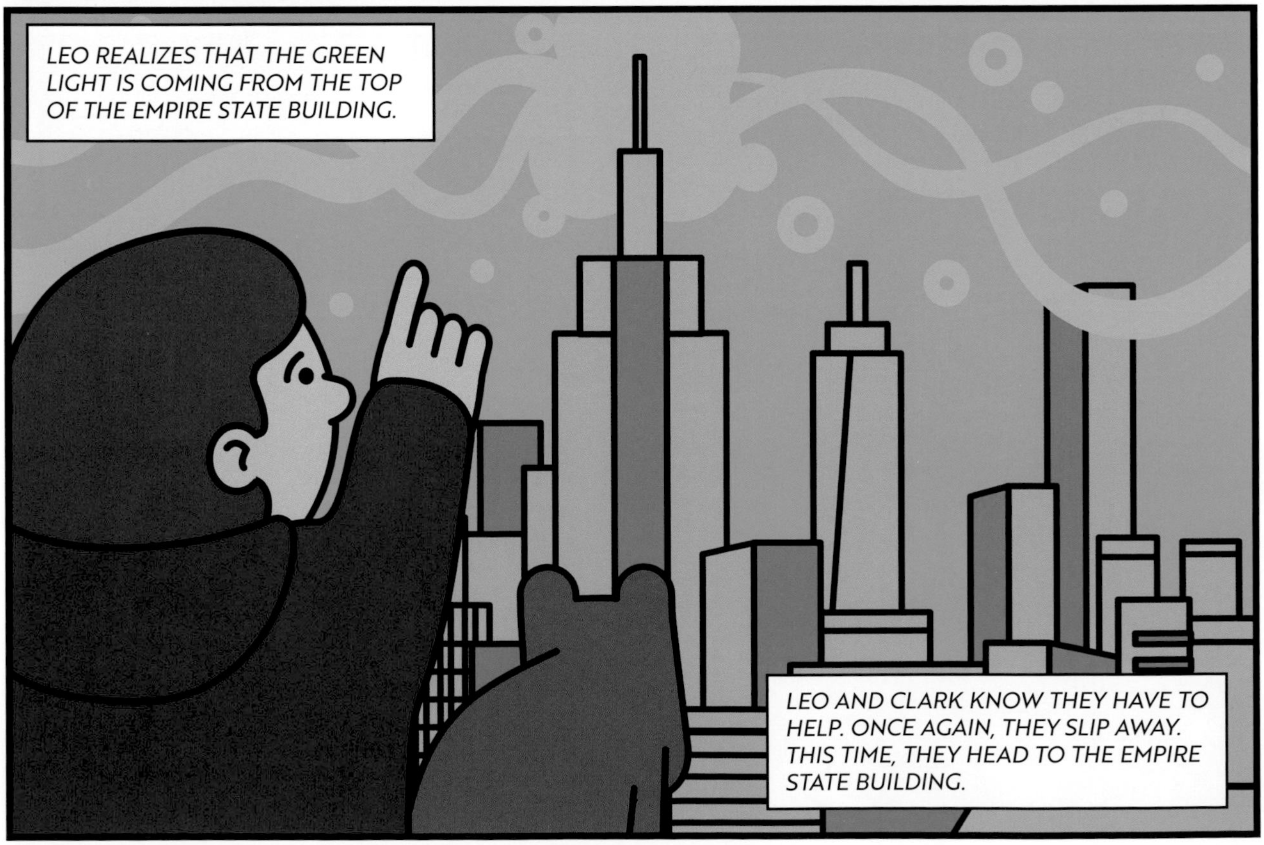
LEO REALIZES THAT THE GREEN LIGHT IS COMING FROM THE TOP OF THE EMPIRE STATE BUILDING.
LEO AND CLARK KNOW THEY HAVE TO HELP. ONCE AGAIN, THEY SLIP AWAY. THIS TIME, THEY HEAD TO THE EMPIRE STATE BUILDING.

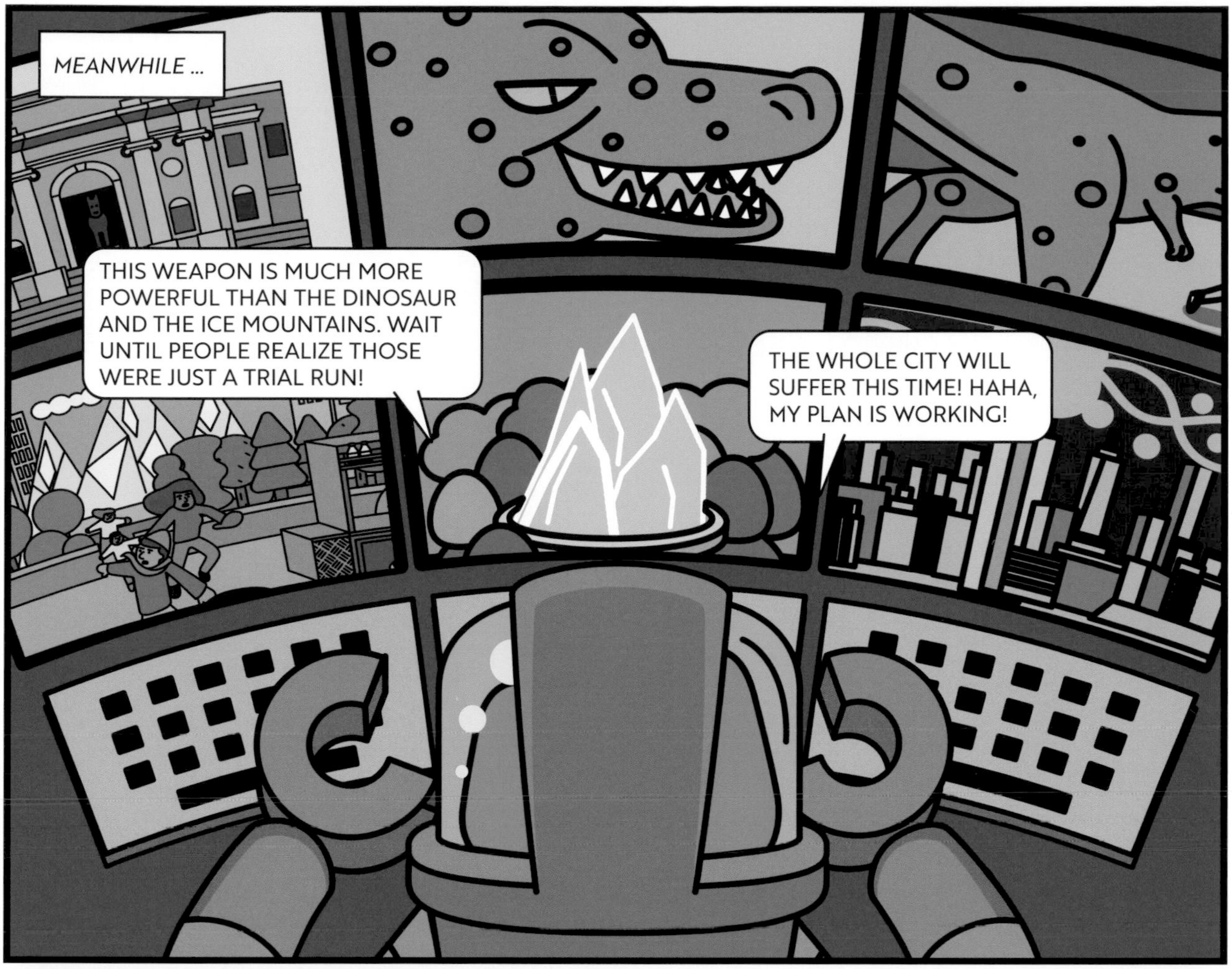
MEANWHILE ...
THIS WEAPON IS MUCH MORE POWERFUL THAN THE DINOSAUR AND THE ICE MOUNTAINS. WAIT UNTIL PEOPLE REALIZE THOSE WERE JUST A TRIAL RUN!
THE WHOLE CITY WILL SUFFER THIS TIME! HAHA, MY PLAN IS WORKING!

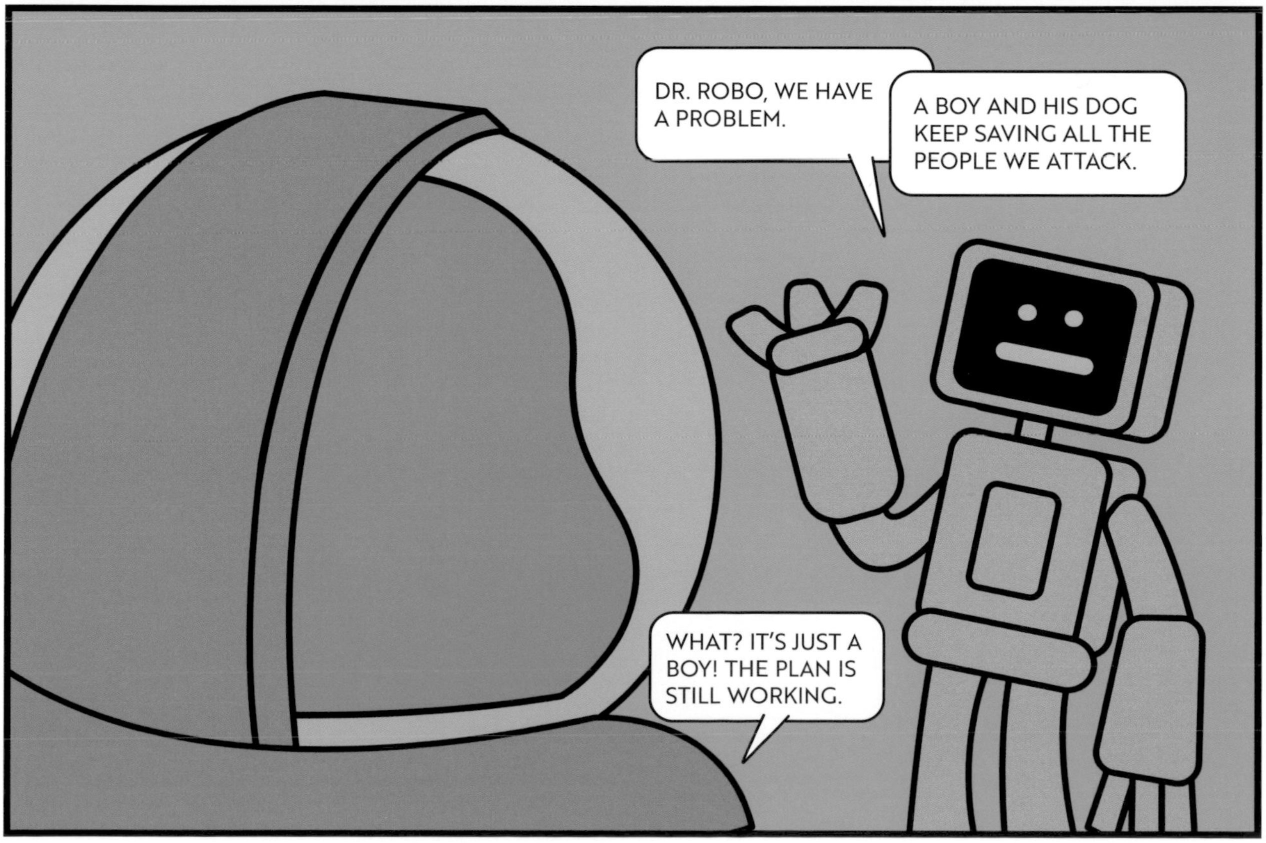
DR. ROBO, WE HAVE A PROBLEM.
A BOY AND HIS DOG KEEP SAVING ALL THE PEOPLE WE ATTACK.
WHAT? IT'S JUST A BOY! THE PLAN IS STILL WORKING.

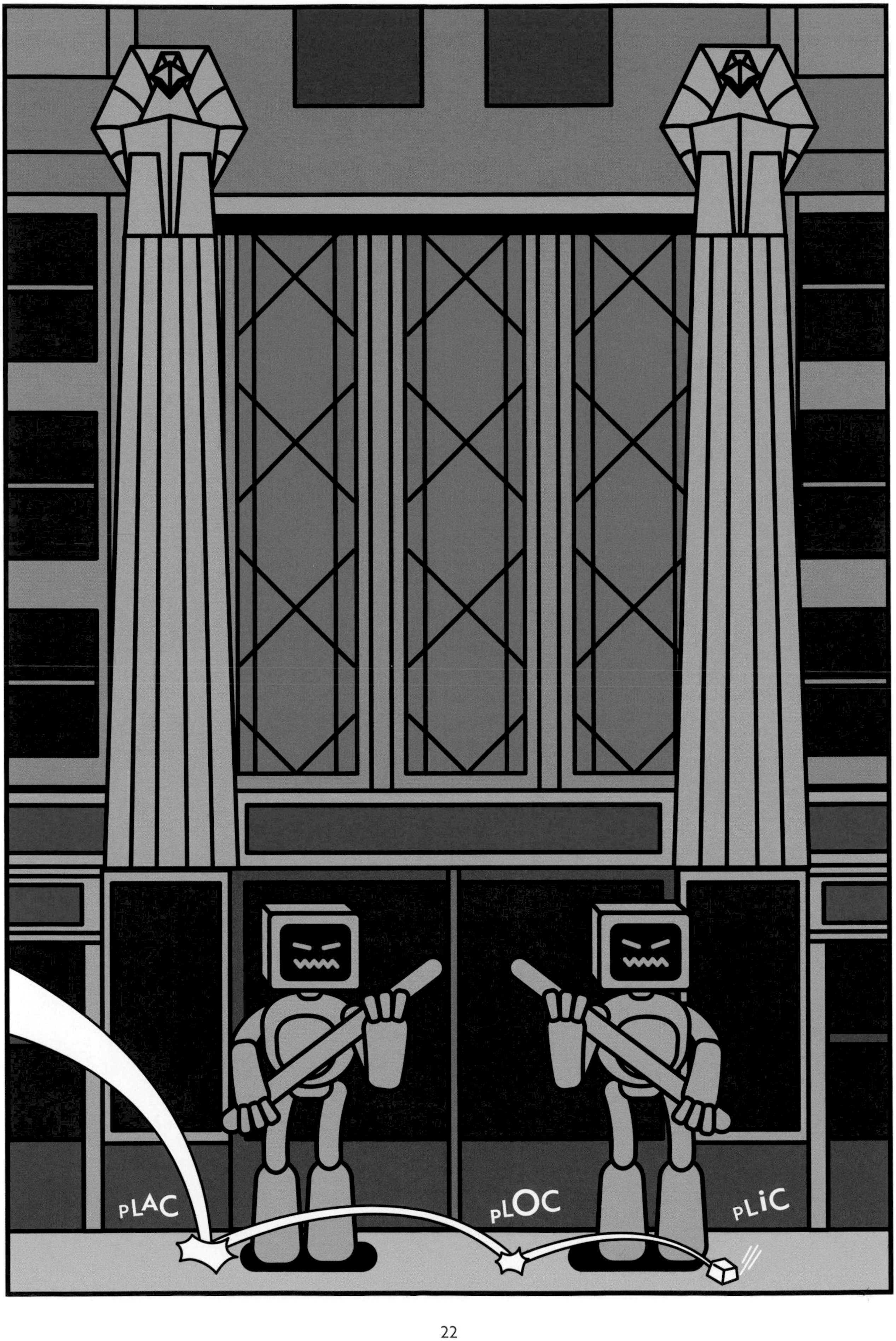
PLAC
PLOC
PLIC

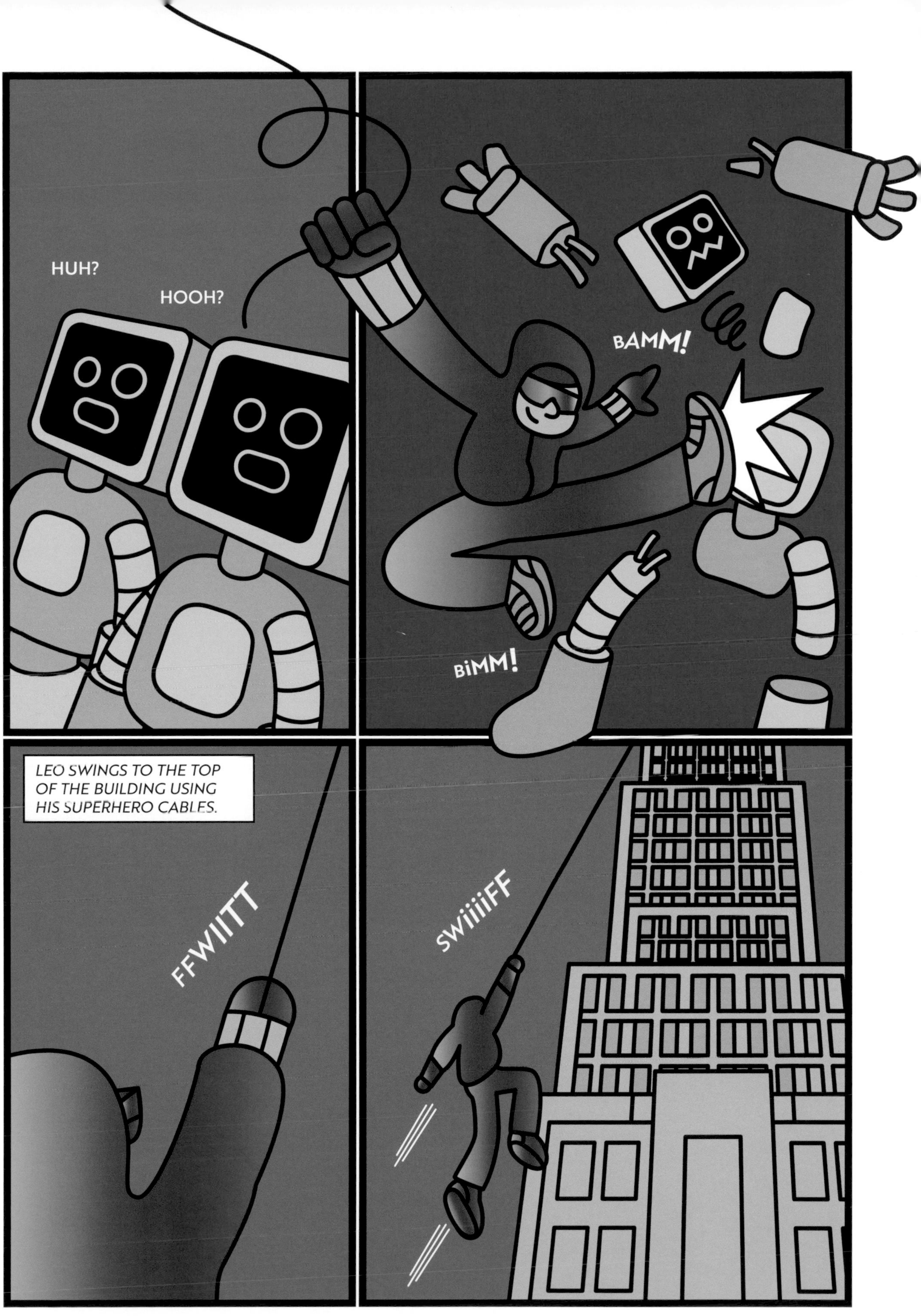
HUH?
HOOH?
BAMM!
BiMM!
LEO SWINGS TO THE TOP OF THE BUILDING USING HIS SUPERHERO CABLES.
FFWIITT
SWiiiiFF

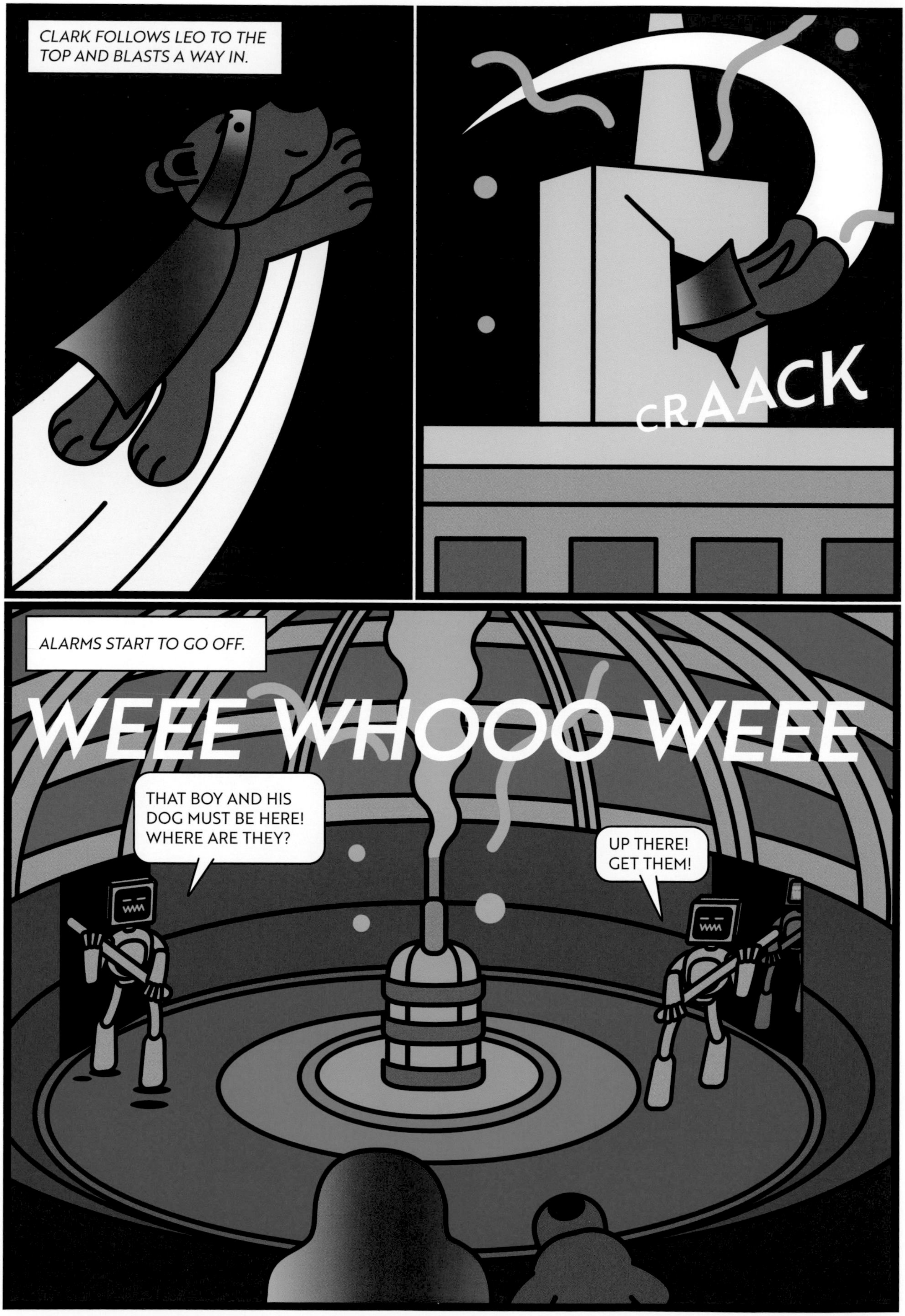
CLARK FOLLOWS LEO TO THE TOP AND BLASTS A WAY IN.
CRAACK
ALARMS START TO GO OFF.
WEEE WHOOO WEEE
THAT BOY AND HIS DOG MUST BE HERE! WHERE ARE THEY?
UP THERE! GET THEM!

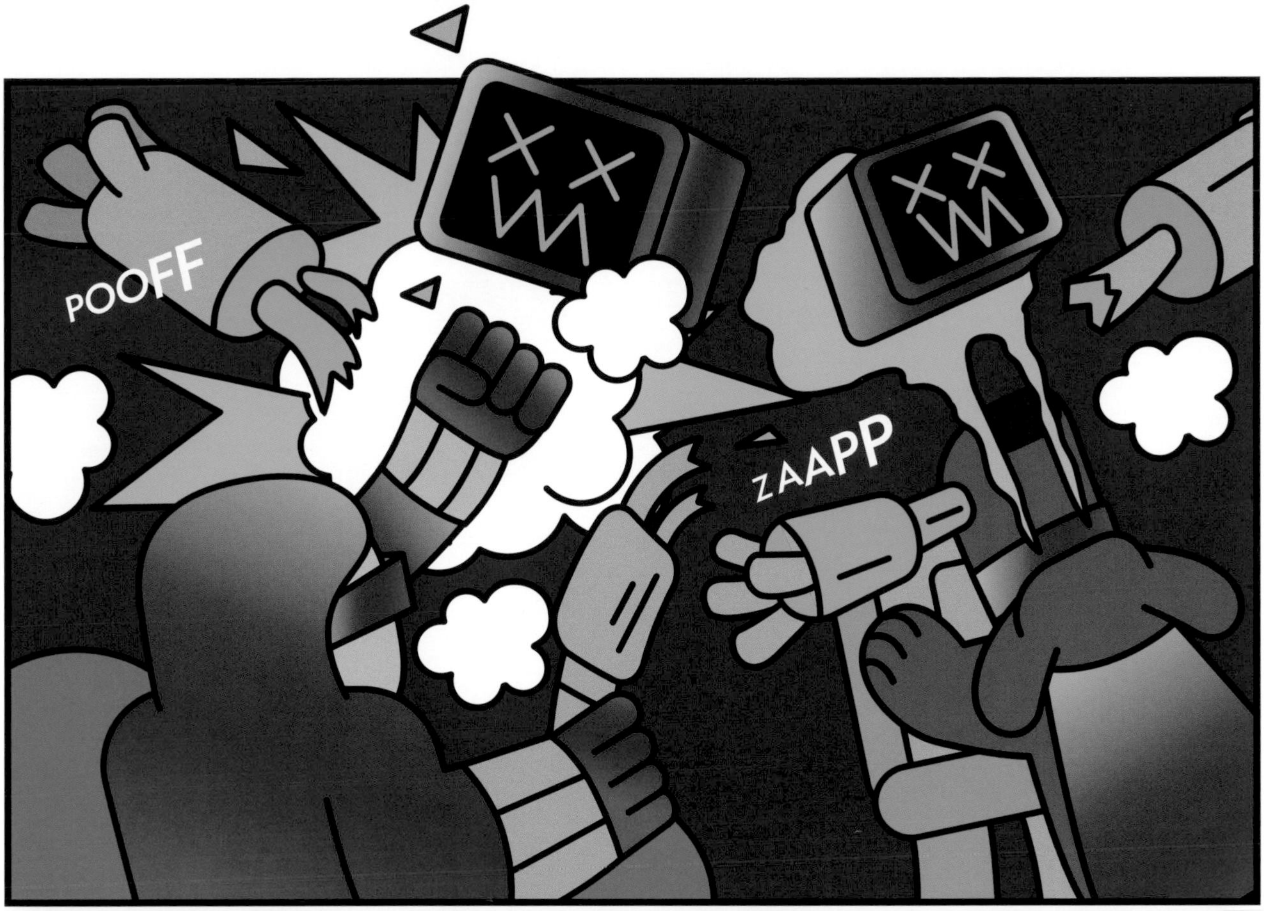
POOFF
ZAAPP

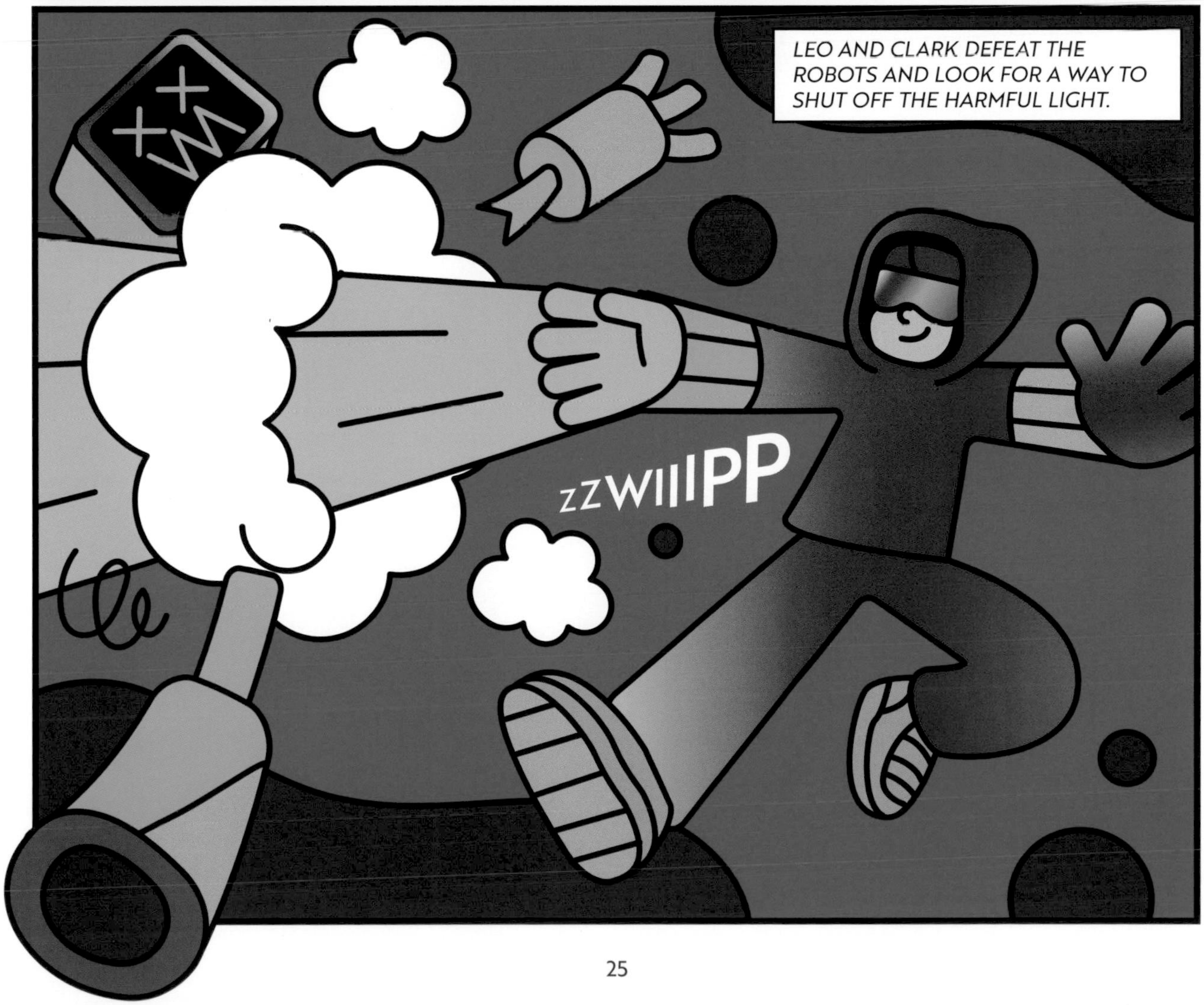
LEO AND CLARK DEFEAT THE ROBOTS AND LOOK FOR A WAY TO SHUT OFF THE HARMFUL LIGHT.
ZZWIIIIPP

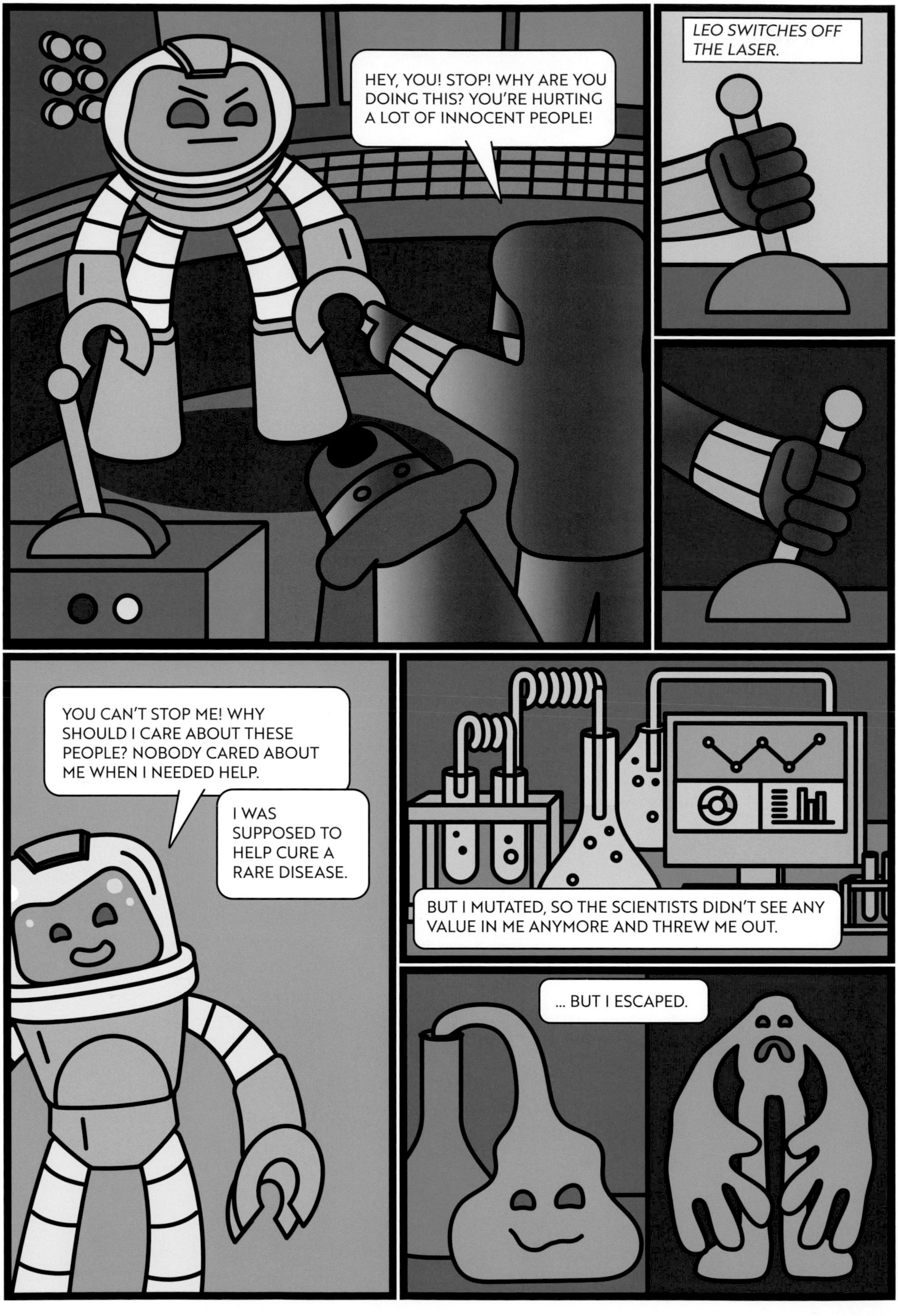
HEY, YOU! STOP! WHY ARE YOU DOING THIS? YOU'RE HURTING A LOT OF INNOCENT PEOPLE!
LEO SWITCHES OFF THE LASER.
YOU CAN'T STOP ME! WHY SHOULD I CARE ABOUT THESE PEOPLE? NOBODY CARED ABOUT ME WHEN I NEEDED HELP.
I WAS SUPPOSED TO HELP CURE A RARE DISEASE.
BUT I MUTATED, SO THE SCIENTISTS DIDN'T SEE ANY VALUE IN ME ANYMORE AND THREW ME OUT.
... BUT I ESCAPED.

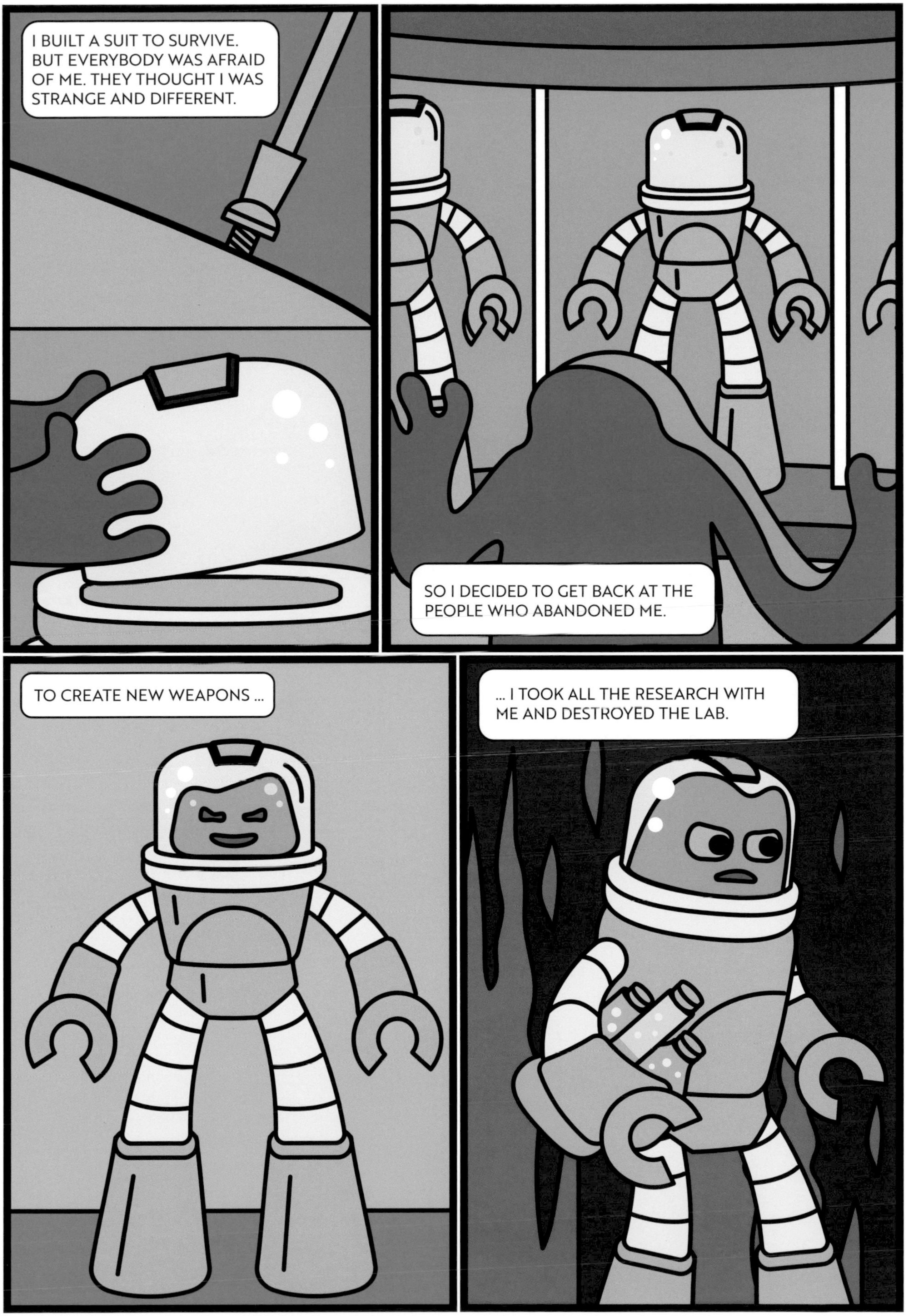
I BUILT A SUIT TO SURVIVE. BUT EVERYBODY WAS AFRAID OF ME. THEY THOUGHT I WAS STRANGE AND DIFFERENT.
SO I DECIDED TO GET BACK AT THE PEOPLE WHO ABANDONED ME.
TO CREATE NEW WEAPONS ...
... I TOOK ALL THE RESEARCH WITH ME AND DESTROYED THE LAB.

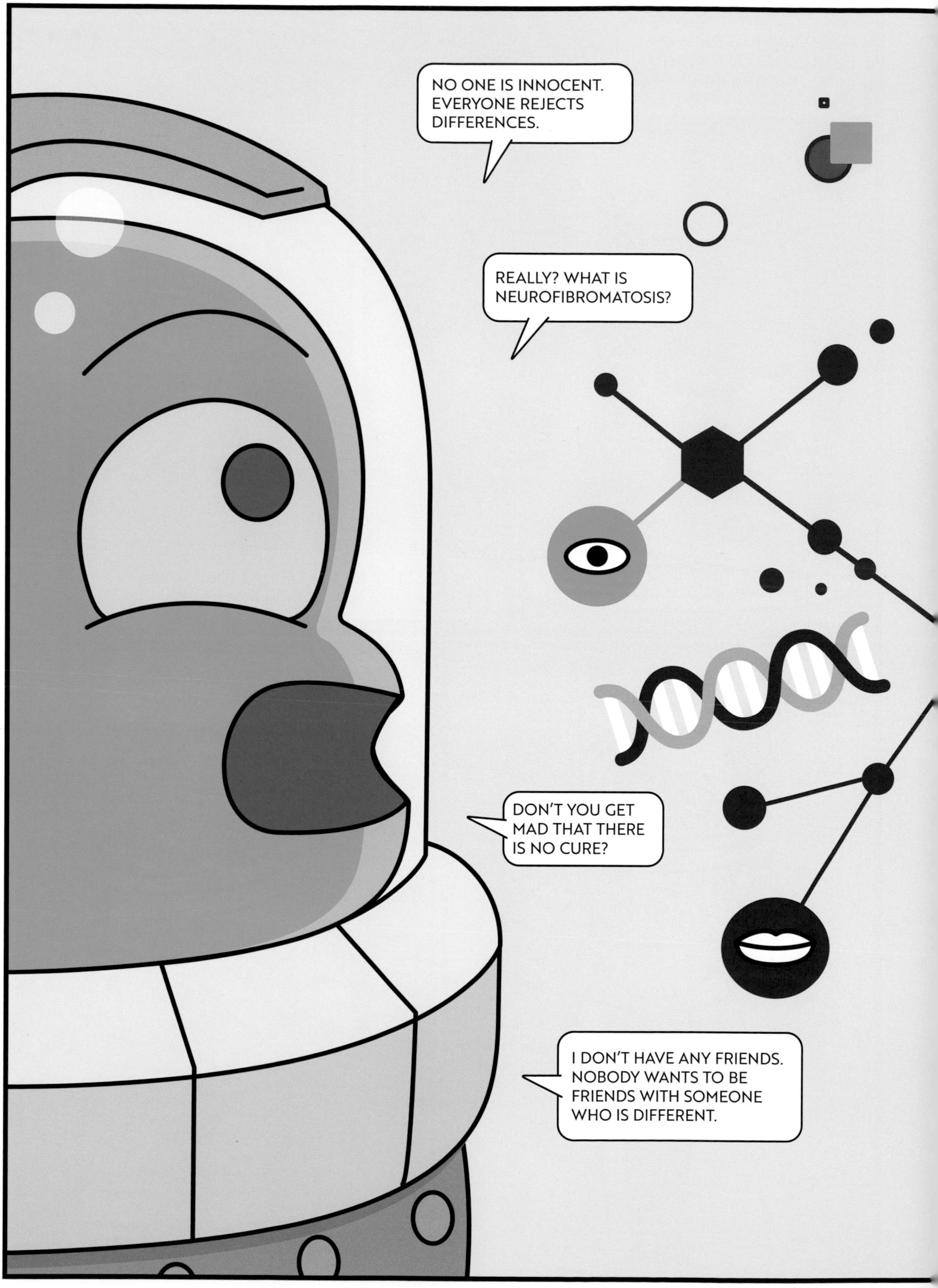
NO ONE IS INNOCENT. EVERYONE REJECTS DIFFERENCES.
REALLY? WHAT IS NEUROFIBROMATOSIS?
DON'T YOU GET MAD THAT THERE IS NO CURE?
I DON'T HAVE ANY FRIENDS. NOBODY WANTS TO BE FRIENDS WITH SOMEONE WHO IS DIFFERENT.

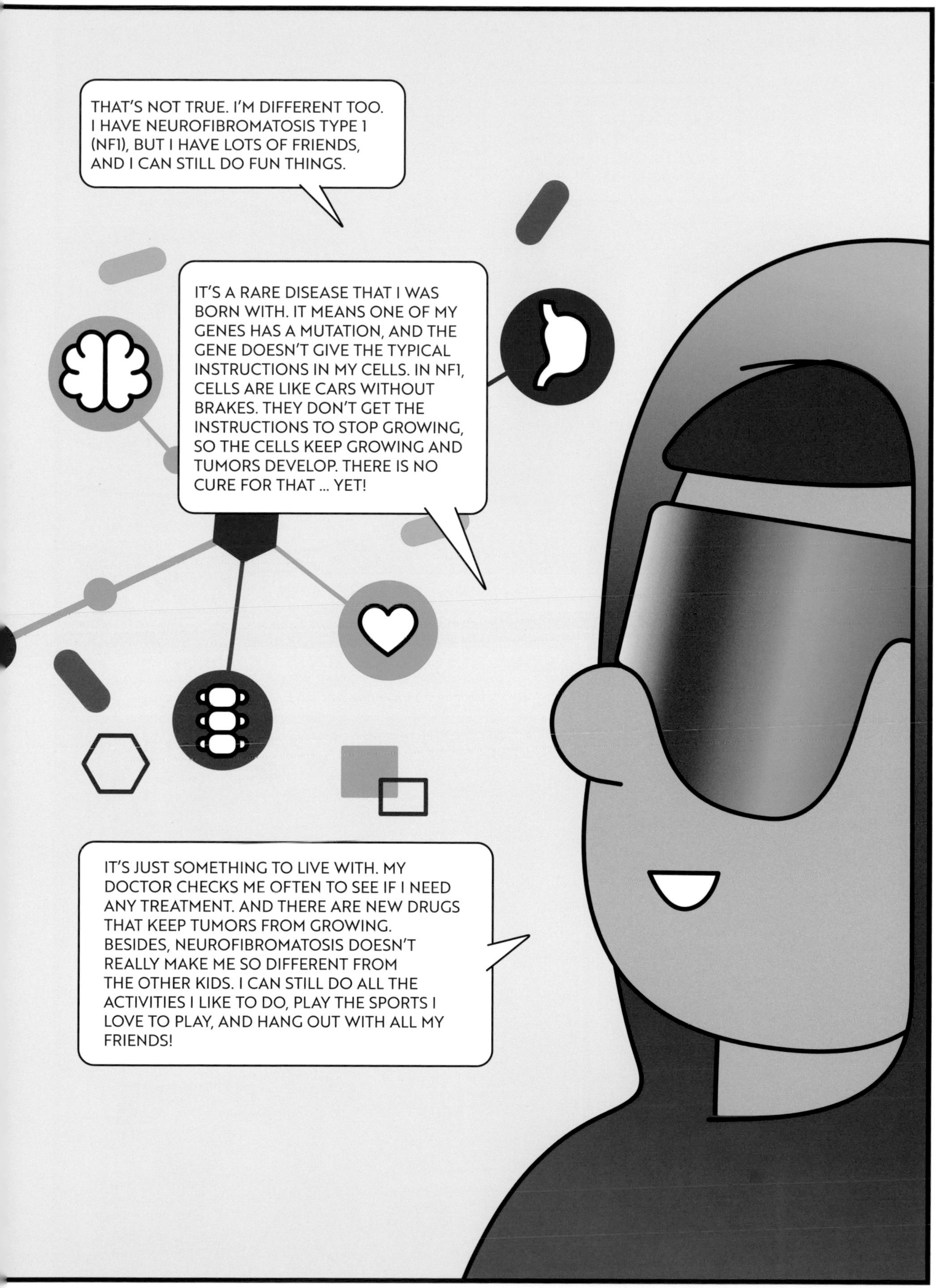
THAT'S NOT TRUE. I'M DIFFERENT TOO. I HAVE NEUROFIBROMATOSIS TYPE 1 (NF1), BUT I HAVE LOTS OF FRIENDS, AND I CAN STILL DO FUN THINGS.
IT'S A RARE DISEASE THAT I WAS BORN WITH. IT MEANS ONE OF MY GENES HAS A MUTATION, AND THE GENE DOESN'T GIVE THE TYPICAL INSTRUCTIONS IN MY CELLS. IN NF1, CELLS ARE LIKE CARS WITHOUT BRAKES. THEY DON'T GET THE INSTRUCTIONS TO STOP GROWING, SO THE CELLS KEEP GROWING AND TUMORS DEVELOP. THERE IS NO CURE FOR THAT ... YET!
IT'S JUST SOMETHING TO LIVE WITH. MY DOCTOR CHECKS ME OFTEN TO SEE IF I NEED ANY TREATMENT. AND THERE ARE NEW DRUGS THAT KEEP TUMORS FROM GROWING. BESIDES, NEUROFIBROMATOSIS DOESN'T REALLY MAKE ME SO DIFFERENT FROM THE OTHER KIDS. I CAN STILL DO ALL THE ACTIVITIES I LIKE TO DO, PLAY THE SPORTS I LOVE TO PLAY, AND HANG OUT WITH ALL MY FRIENDS!

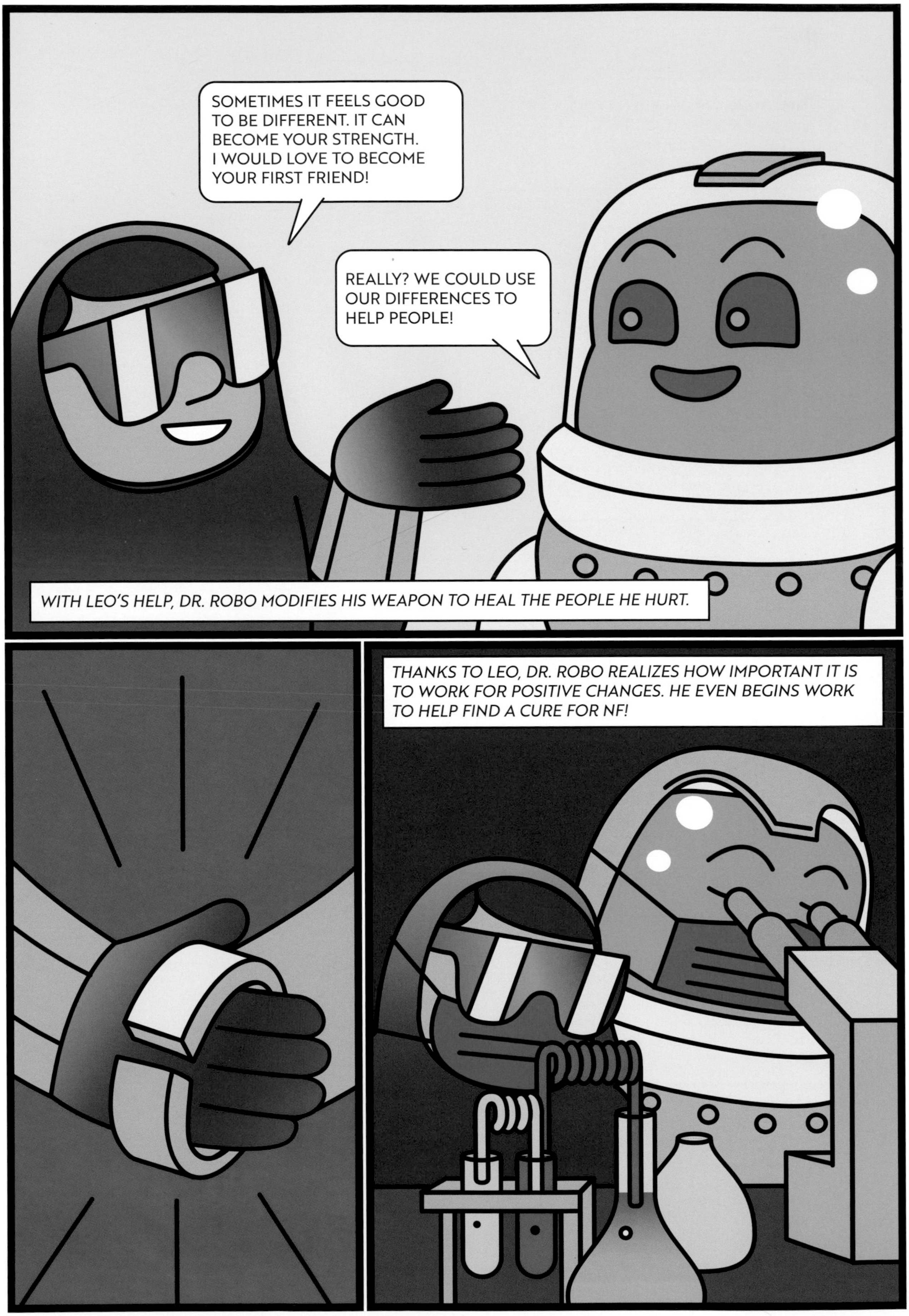
SOMETIMES IT FEELS GOOD TO BE DIFFERENT. IT CAN BECOME YOUR STRENGTH. I WOULD LOVE TO BECOME YOUR FIRST FRIEND!
REALLY? WE COULD USE OUR DIFFERENCES TO HELP PEOPLE!
WITH LEO'S HELP, DR. ROBO MODIFIES HIS WEAPON TO HEAL THE PEOPLE HE HURT.
THANKS TO LEO, DR. ROBO REALIZES HOW IMPORTANT IT IS TO WORK FOR POSITIVE CHANGES. HE EVEN BEGINS WORK TO HELP FIND A CURE FOR NF!

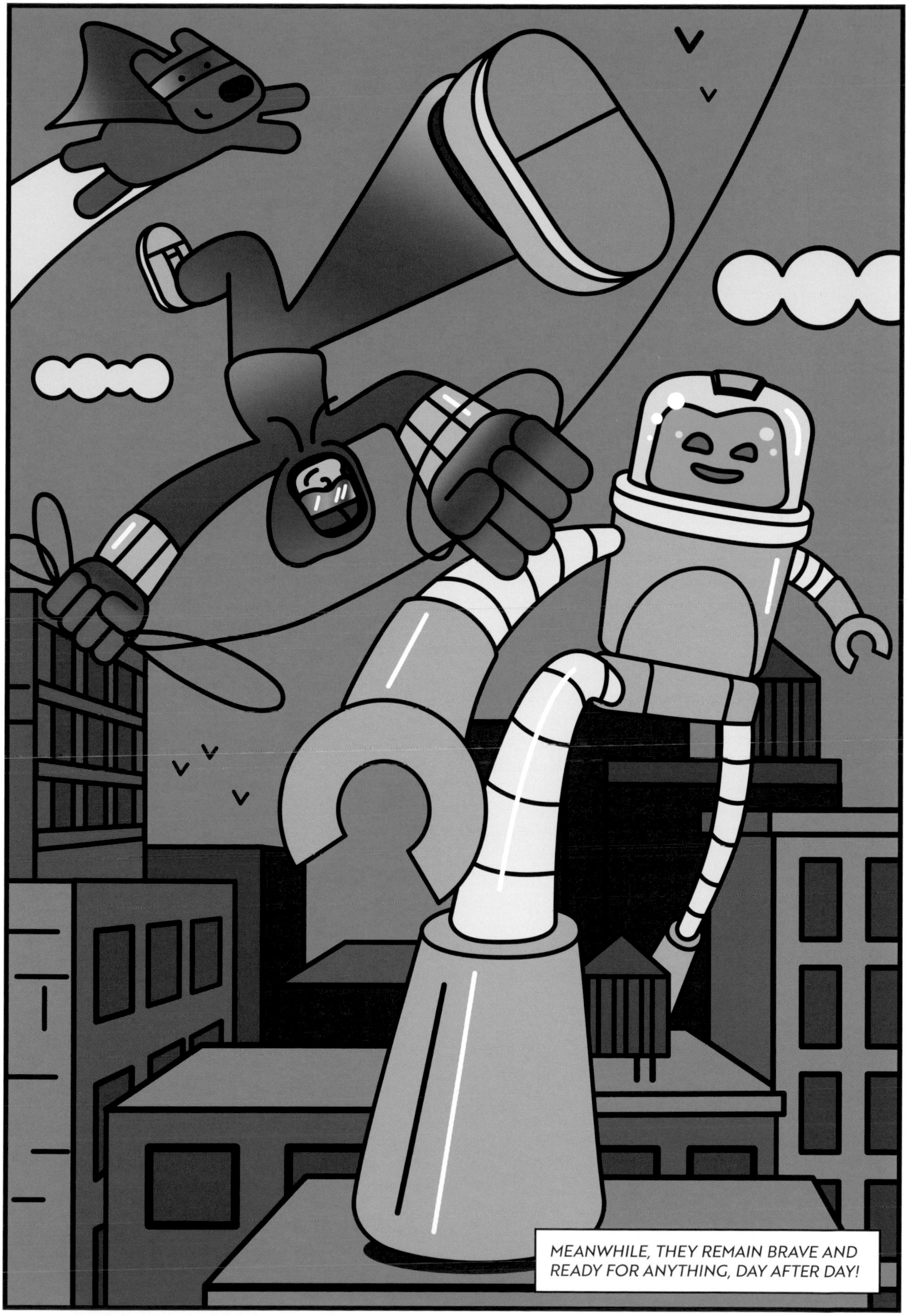
MEANWHILE, THEY REMAIN BRAVE AND
READY FOR ANYTHING, DAY AFTER DAY!

KEY TERMS

café au lait macules: flat brown spots on skin that people with NF1 develop during childhood

chromosomes: tightly coiled strands of DNA that are made up of segments called genes and stored in the core (nucleus) of a cell

gene: a segment of DNA that determines a specific trait, such as eye or hair color, and is passed from parent to child

neurofibroma: harmless (benign) tumor that forms around nerves

optic glioma: growth on the eye nerve that can cause problems with vision

scoliosis: curving of the spine

tumor suppressor gene: gene that prevents uncontrolled growth of cells and tumor formation

MORE INFORMATION FROM THE MEDICAL EDITOR

By **Dusica Babovic-Vuksanovic, M.D.**
Consultant, Department of Clinical Genomics, Mayo Clinic, Rochester, MN, Jacksonville, FL;
Professor of Medical Genetics and Pediatrics, Mayo Clinic College of Medicine and Science

Neurofibromatosis type 1 (NF1) is an inherited (genetic) disorder that affects about 1 in 3,000 people. It is caused by changes (mutations) in the NF1 **gene**, a **tumor suppressor gene**. Only one parent needs to pass on the **gene** with these mutations to cause the disease.

Most people with NF1 develop flat skin spots called **café au lait macules**. It's also common to have freckling in the armpit, groin and neck and brown spots on the colorful part of the eye (iris), known as Lisch nodules. At some point during life, almost everyone with NF1 will have soft, pea-sized bumps (tumors) on or under the skin called **neurofibromas**. Less common signs of NF1 include problems with bone development such as a curved spine (**scoliosis**) or bowed lower leg.

People with NF1 have an increased risk of brain tumors. Tumors on the optic nerve (**optic gliomas**) may form in childhood, while a type of tumor called a glioblastoma appears more often in older age. **Neurofibromas** that form on nerves outside the brain and spinal cord need close monitoring, because some can become cancerous. Children with NF1 also may have learning disabilities, attention deficit/hyperactivity disorder, and problems with behavior or social adjustment.

Treatment of NF1 involves frequent doctor visits to look for early complications. Speech therapy, occupational therapy, physical therapy and behavioral interventions can help improve daily life for people with NF1. In addition, a new medication may help children with NF1 form fewer tumors that involve many nerves (plexiform **neurofibromas**). The medication targets the cellular process that causes this type of tumor. More clinical studies are ongoing. Researchers hope to develop treatment for other complications of NF1 — and, eventually, a cure.

REFERENCES

Miller DT, Freedenberg D, Schorry E, Ullrich NJ, Viskochil D, Korf BR; Council on Genetics; American College of Medical Genetics and Genomics. Health Supervision for Children with Neurofibromatosis Type 1. Pediatrics. 2019 May;143(5):e20190660. doi: 10.1542/peds.2019-0660. PMID: 31010905.

Legius E, Messiaen L, Wolkenstein P, Pancza P, Avery RA, Berman Y, Blakeley J, Babovic-Vuksanovic D, Cunha KS, Ferner R, Fisher MJ, Friedman JM, Gutmann DH, Kehrer-Sawatzki H, Korf BR, Mautner VF, Peltonen S, Rauen KA, Riccardi V, Schorry E, Stemmer-Rachamimov A, Stevenson DA, Tadini G, Ullrich NJ, Viskochil D, Wimmer K, Yohay K; International Consensus Group on Neurofibromatosis Diagnostic Criteria (I-NF-DC), Huson SM, Evans DG, Plotkin SR. Revised diagnostic criteria for neurofibromatosis type 1 and Legius syndrome: an international consensus recommendation. Genet Med. 2021 Aug;23(8):1506-1513. doi: 10.1038/s41436-021-01170-5. Epub 2021 May 19. PMID: 34012067; PMCID: PMC8354850.

Legius E, Brems H. Genetic basis of neurofibromatosis type 1 and related conditions, including mosaicism. Childs Nerv Syst. 2020 Oct;36(10):2285-2295. doi: 10.1007/s00381-020-04771-8. Epub 2020 Jun 29. PMID: 32601904.

Mensink KA, Ketterling RP, Flynn HC, Knudson RA, Lindor NM, Heese BA, Spinner RJ, Babovic-Vuksanovic D. Connective tissue dysplasia in five new patients with NF1 microdeletions: further expansion of phenotype and review of the literature. J Med Genet. 2006 Feb;43(2):e8. doi: 10.1136/jmg.2005.034256. PMID: 16467218; PMCID: PMC2603036.

WEB RESOURCES

Children's Tumor Foundation — www.ctf.org
The Children's Tumor Foundation's mission is to drive research, expand knowledge and advance care for the NF community.

Neurofibromatosis Network — www.nfnetwork.org
The Neurofibromatosis Network is a nonprofit organization that aims to find treatments and a cure for neurofibromatosis by promoting scientific research, improving clinical care, providing outreach through education and awareness, while offering hope and support to those affected by NF.

NF North Central — nfnorthcentral.nfnetwork.org
NF North Central's mission is to work to authentically educate, advocate, counsel, support and fund research initiatives benefitting those impacted by neurofibromatosis.

ABOUT THE MEDICAL EDITOR

By **Dusica Babovic-Vuksanovic, M.D.**
Consultant, Department of Clinical Genomics, Mayo Clinic, Rochester, MN, Jacksonville, FL;
Professor of Medical Genetics and Pediatrics, Mayo Clinic College of Medicine and Science
Dr. Babovic-Vuksanovic is a pediatrician and clinical researcher in genetics at Mayo Clinic and is the director of Mayo's Neurofibromatosis Clinic. She leads several collaborative studies looking at children, adolescents and young adults with neurofibromatosis type 1 and progressive plexiform **neurofibromas** as well as adult patients with neurofibromatosis type 1 and extensive plexiform and paraspinal **neurofibromas**. Dr. Babovic-Vuksanovic is passionate in her work toward a better understanding of various genetic syndromes and metabolic disorders, aiming to improve diagnosis, treatment and outcomes for patients with these conditions.

ABOUT THE AUTHORS

Guillaume Federighi, aka **Hey Gee**, is a French and American author and illustrator. He began his career in 1998 in Paris, France. He also spent a few decades exploring the world of street art and graffiti in different European capitals. After moving to New York in 2008, he worked with many companies and brands, developing a reputation in graphic design and illustration for his distinctive style of translating complex ideas into simple and timeless visual stories.
He is also the owner and creative director of Hey Gee Studio, a full-service creative agency based in New York City.

G.W. Page was diagnosed with a rare genetic condition called neurofibromatosis (NF) as a baby, after his mom noticed some new birthmark-type spots on his legs. When he was 3 years old, an MRI revealed a large tumor in G.W.'s brain, requiring surgery to remove it. Now at age 10, G.W. has an extensive team of doctors who routinely monitor him for new tumors or other NF-related problems, which can be very unpredictable. With his positive outlook and fierce courage, even as the youngest of his siblings, he sets a big example for his family about choosing how to react when things go wrong or when they are afraid. He loves playing sports, creating art, fishing, fantasy football, cooking with his dad, and being a goofball with his big sisters. When he grows up, G.W. hopes to become a professional sports analyst.

ABOUT FONDATION IPSEN BOOKLAB

Fondation Ipsen improves the lives of millions of people around the world by rethinking scientific communication. The truthful transmission of science to the public is complex because scientific information is often technical and there is a lot of inaccurate information. In 2018, Fondation Ipsen established BookLab to address this need. BookLab books come about through collaboration between scientists, doctors, artists, authors, and children. In paper and electronic formats, and in several languages, BookLab delivers books across more than 50 countries for people of all ages and cultures. Fondation Ipsen BookLab's publications are free of charge to schools, libraries and people living in precarious situations. Join us! Access and share our books by visiting: www.fondation-ipsen.org.

ABOUT MAYO CLINIC PRESS

Launched in 2019, Mayo Clinic Press shines a light on the most fascinating stories in medicine and empowers individuals with the knowledge to build healthier, happier lives. From the award-winning *Mayo Clinic Health Letter* to books and media covering the scope of human health and wellness, Mayo Clinic Press publications provide readers with reliable and trusted content by some of the world's leading health care professionals. Proceeds benefit important medical research and education at Mayo Clinic. For more information about Mayo Clinic Press, visit MCPress.MayoClinic.org.

ABOUT THE COLLABORATION

The My Life Beyond series was developed in partnership between Fondation Ipsen's BookLab and Mayo Clinic, which has provided world-class medical education for more than 150 years. This collaboration aims to provide trustworthy, impactful resources for understanding childhood diseases and other problems that can affect children's well-being.

The series offers readers a holistic perspective of children's lives with — and beyond — their medical challenges. In creating these books, young people who have been Mayo Clinic patients worked together with author-illustrator Hey Gee, sharing their personal experiences. The resulting fictionalized stories authentically bring to life the patients' emotions and their inspiring responses to challenging circumstances. In addition, Mayo Clinic physicians contributed the latest medical expertise on each topic so that these stories can best help other patients, families and caregivers understand how children perceive and work through their own challenges.

Text: Hey Gee and G.W. Page
Illustrations: Hey Gee

Medical editor: Dusica Babovic-Vuksanovic, M.D.
Consultant, Department Clinical Genomics, Mayo Clinic, Rochester, MN, MN, Jacksonville, FL;
Professor of Medical Genetics and Pediatrics, Mayo Clinic College of Medicine and Science

Managing editor: Anna Cavallo, Health Education and Content Services/Mayo Clinic Press, Mayo Clinic, Rochester, MN
Project manager: Kim Chandler, Department of Education, Mayo Clinic, Rochester, MN
Manager of publications: Céline Colombier-Maffre, Fondation Ipsen, Paris, France
President: James A. Levine, M.D., Ph.D., Professor, Fondation Ipsen, Paris, France

MAYO CLINIC PRESS
200 First St. SW
Rochester, MN 55905
mcpress.mayoclinic.org

For bulk sales to employers, member groups and health-related companies, contact Mayo Clinic, 200 First St. SW, Rochester, MN 55905, or send an email to SpecialSalesMayoBooks@mayo.edu.

Proceeds from the sale of every book benefit important medical research and education at Mayo Clinic.

ISBN 978-1-945564-06-2

Library of Congress Control Number: 2021950927

Printed in the United States of America

Logos of the Neurofibromatosis Network appearing on page 18 are used with permission.